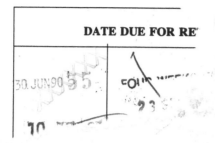

Critical Guides to French Texts

72 Lesage: Gil Blas

Critical Guides to French Texts

EDITED BY ROGER LITTLE, WOLFGANG VAN EMDEN,
DAVID WILLIAMS

LESAGE

Gil Blas

Malcolm Cook

Senior Lecturer in French,
University of Exeter

Grant & Cutler Ltd
1988

333481

I.S.B.N. 84-599-2549-8

DEPÓSITO LEGAL: V. 2.635 - 1988

Printed in Spain by
Artes Gráficas Soler, S. A., Valencia

for

GRANT & CUTLER LTD
55-57 GREAT MARLBOROUGH STREET, LONDON W1V 2AY

Contents

Preface   9

Introduction: Narrative Perspectives and Problems
    of Interpretation   11

1 *Gil Blas* – a Picaresque Novel?   15

2 Structure I: the Significance of Minor Characters   20

3 Structure II: the Interpolated Stories   31

4 Novel Form: Qualities and Defects   36

5 A Comic Novel   45

6 The Character of Gil   59

7 *Gil Blas* and Meaning   64

8 Conclusion   71

Select Bibliography   73

For Odile, S. F. and D.

Preface

G IL B L A S, one of the most successful of eighteenth-century
French novels, presents the reader with a demanding chal-
lenge. Many students are overawed by the sheer length of the
text and, as a consequence, many teachers have been accom-
plices to the disappearance of *Gil Blas* from anything but
highly specialised courses. *Gil Blas* is not the sort of text that
lends itself to the examination system. It is a huge compendium of ideas, of borrowings, of comedy and of satire. It is,
foremost, a comic novel, and it is my contention that the
comedy must be the unifying factor in the text. But the nature
of the comedy is various and diverse – and I shall try, in this
short study, to emphasise this aspect in preference to others.
Lesage borrowed willingly, and at length, from many authors. Voltaire accused him of plagiarism, with some justification. It is not my task to analyse the extent of borrowings
– indeed, two recent studies are better equipped to cope with
them (see *2* and *6*). I will assume, for critical convenience,
that Lesage is sole author and that the text is a uniform one. I
will assume that *Gil Blas* is a long novel and not spend undue
time treating the three different *livraisons* – the text appeared
over a long period of time: Books I-VI appearing in 1715,
Books VII-IX in 1724, and Books X-XII in 1735. Obviously,
not all the readers of the first and second *livraisons* would
have been alive to see the conclusion in Book XII. It was not
unusual, in the eighteenth century, for novels to appear over
a period of years. Some novels were never completed – one
thinks of Marivaux's *La Vie de Marianne* of 1731-41 and of
his *Paysan parvenu* of 1734-35, both of which were left
apparently unfinished. It is not the conclusion of the novels
which represents their greatest interest. Lesage's rambling,

account of Gil's social ascension is enjoyable not because of
what happens at the end, but because of what happens on the
way. Many of my students have reacted against the interpolated stories, saying that they get in the way and that they
distract our attention from the main character. My response
to that criticism is that they are taking the main character too
seriously and that they should enjoy the interludes for their
own sake.

Gil Blas belongs to a literary tradition that the 'realist'
novels of the nineteenth century have tended to make us
forget. Gil himself represents the frame of a *roman à tiroirs*
where characters are introduced and tell their own stories. It
is possible, on occasions, to draw parallels between the main
body of the text and its interpolated stories, but this is not my
primary concern.

My intention is to facilitate the task of reading a long,
complex novel by pointing out its qualities and its defects, by
criticising, in the broadest sense, so that modern students can
face the daunting prospect of 609 pages of text with pleasure
and amusement. I have, as far as possible, kept strictly to the
text. This obviously limits the discussion of sources and of
parody and for this I apologise in advance. Interested readers
will not read *Gil Blas* in isolation but will refer to Lesage's
borrowings and imitations and consider for themselves their
import. Laufer's edition is well annotated and provides ample
details for further reading.

All references to the text are from Roger Laufer's edition
(Paris, Garnier-Flammarion, 1977). This edition contains a
chronology of Lesage's life, pp. 5-6, and a short but useful
Introduction, pp. 7-14. Laufer chooses the revised 1715
edition of Books I-VI, the 1724 edition of Books VII-IX and
the revised 1735 edition of Books X-XII. References to works
listed in the Select Bibliography give the number of the work
in italics, followed by the page numbers, thus: *10,* pp. 123-37.

Introduction: Narrative Perspectives and Problems of Interpretation

I F it is necessary to read the final pages of the novel to understand it, many early readers will have gone to the grave unenlightened. It is clearly possible to assume that the end of Book VI is a conclusion to the novel: Gil Blas has been rewarded by don Alphonse and is now established in a role as 'intendant' – the final words: 'c'était commencer le métier d'intendant par où l'on devrait le finir' (p. 310) form a satisfactory conclusion to the episode and to the volume. If the novel had not been continued, many readers would have felt that the conclusion was a satisfactory one. The 1724 *livraison* cannot be understood without reference to the 1715 one, nor can the 1735 *livraison* without reference to the 1724 one. The novel proceeds in stages so that by the end of Book VI Gil Blas is well established; by the end of Book IX he has learnt a harsh lesson about the nature of power and ambition, and by the end of Book XII he has settled into a peaceful, contented retirement. He leads a 'vie délicieuse' and the progression through life's misfortunes is complete. But how is the reader supposed to approach the text or texts? Is he expected to forget the three publication dates and concentrate on the 'unity' of the whole? Or is he justified in separating the texts and analysing them separately?

While one can, with profit, study simply Books I-VI, as Jean Molino has done (*12*), one must, in fairness, look at the complete text as it evolves. Lesage learns much over twenty years. It is said, by some, that the later books are the work of an ageing man who has lost his verve and who is led into repetition and coincidence. It seems to me that Lesage's perspective changes considerably over twenty years. In the early books the reader is interested essentially in the social

ascension of a naïve young man. The confrontation of youth
and the outside world is a comic one, but the comedy is of an
elementary nature. Gil Blas is tricked by flattery: 'Est-il bien
possible que vous soyez ce savantissime, ce bel esprit dont la
réputation est si grande en ce pays-ci?' (p. 27), he is asked,
but at no time is the reader fooled. We know that Gil Blas
cannot yet conform to the description given of him: the
language of exaggeration is plainly apparent to us, but it was
not to Gil. Yet, if we accept the illusion of the first person
narrator, it must be obvious that Gil, as narrator, is observing
himself with hindsight: he is laughing at himself – or more
precisely, Lesage is mocking his own creation.

As the novel proceeds and Gil gains in experience the
distance between character and reader diminishes. We begin
to identify more clearly with Gil when his misfortunes are
not the result of his own inexperience or stupidity. Lesage
guides us into identification with the character by following
the ageing process. The distance between Gil the character
and Gil the narrator diminishes as time passes. It is through
this narrowing process that the message of the novel becomes
apparent. As I shall show later, progress, power and authority
are not simply the result of merit: chance plays an enormous
part in Gil's progress, and as the tale proceeds, so this fact is
more readily acknowledged by Gil. It is this basic honesty
towards life which, in the end, makes Gil a sympathetic
character. Of course, he learns much about the world as he
grows in experience. But his knowledge never puts him in a
position of undoubted superiority. His position is, even at the
height of his political power, dependent on the whim of one
man – and the demise, first of the duc de Lerme, and then of
d'Olivarès, are sufficient reminders of that.

If the time perspective allows a more sophisticated interpretation, so too does it permit a growing awareness of the
novel form and a clear change of emphasis, especially in the
final books. The *roman à tiroirs* gives way to a more
conventional memoir novel: the comic elements gradually
disappear as the narrator experiences life as an adult and as
his judgement matures. This introduces problems of its own:
the illusion of one man, looking back on his life and relating

events from the distant past moving towards the present is broken by the clear differences between the *livraisons*. Georges May (*11*, p. 55) does not distinguish between the different parts of the novel but claims, with a certain justification: 'le monde qui sert de scène aux aventures de *Gil Blas* témoigne déjà de l'effort fait par Lesage pour suggérer dans son roman la diversité et la complexité du réel'. Jennifer Longhurst (*10*, p. 131) claims that the novel is realistic because it rejects romantic ideals (which I think is questionable) and because there is an absence of supernatural devices. I would like to suggest that the novel is realistic *because* of the narrative perspective. In other words, as the difference between Gil Blas as character and Gil Blas as narrator narrows with the passage of time, so the comedy, which is dependent on distance, tends to disappear and the two positions merge. Gil Blas, at the end, cannot laugh at himself any more because he, now, *is* himself.

Vivienne Mylne has pointed out that Lesage is weak in his presentation of deep emotion (*14*, pp. 52-53). I think one can go further and say that the weakness can be related to the narrative position. It is easy for Gil to be ironic and witty about his distant self. It is less easy to detach oneself from the recent past, and the one moment of true sadness, the deaths of Antonia, his first wife, and their son (p. 538), is described with alarming brevity. The apparent lack of emotion may conceal the very opposite: 'je tombai dans un accablement stupide; à force de sentir la perte que je faisais, j'y paraissais comme insensible'. Gil never recovers from this tragic incident and the death of doña Maria, daughter of d'Olivarès (p. 559) is a painful reminder: 'Il faut dire la vérité, je me servis de cette occasion pour donner de nouvelles larmes à la mémoire d'Antonia' (p. 559).

Critics have seen *Gil Blas* as a fusion of different kinds of novel: Showalter (*19*, p. 136) accuses Lesage, somewhat unfairly, of having no artistic vision of reality, and of technical incompetence. It would be easy to say that *Gil Blas* has something for everybody but this would be a disservice to the novel. What I am suggesting is that the narrative position or, more precisely, the narrative positions, convey the meaning

of the novel. Lesage is a more subtle, more aware novelist
than he is normally given credit for. He is progressively more
aware of the evolution of his own text – even to the point of
self-consciousness.

1

Gil Blas – a Picaresque Novel?

M A N Y critics have spent much time trying to decide whether or not *Gil Blas* is a picaresque novel. It is a problem which should not trouble the reader unduly and it is certainly not one to bother the casual reader. I suspect that the question can best be approached from a different angle: rather than compare *Gil Blas* with the traditional picaresque, it might be more profitable to ask why Lesage should want to give his account a Spanish flavour.

There are certain expectations in the picaresque novel, but the most significant are related to the nature of the main character, the *pícaro*. The *pícaro* is often a rogue relating his adventures; he is born of poor and dishonest parents who are often unmarried; he has to serve to survive and flits from master to master, each of whom he outwits and describes in the interests of satire.[1] It seems to me that *Gil Blas* is often treated as an example of the 'picaresque' simply because the action takes place in Spain. Certainly, if we consider that the defining narrative position of the form is the hero, then *Gil Blas* is not a picaresque novel. Moreover, it seems to me, Lesage tries hard to make the reader accept such a view by deliberately distancing his hero – or anti-hero – from more obvious *pícaros* in the text – such as don Raphaël or, even better, Scipion. Admittedly, Scipion does not enter the novel until Book VIII, at a crucial moment in the development: Gil has succeeded the unfortunate don Valerio as secretary to the duc de Lerme and the duc asks Gil for an account of his life.

[1] See H. Sieber, *The Picaresque* (London, Methuen, The Critical Idiom, 33, 1977).

Gil is a little embarrassed at showing himself naked, as it were, in front of his new powerful employer so, he admits: 'Je pris le parti de farder la vérité dans les endroits où elle aurait fait peur toute nue. Mais il ne laissa pas de la démêler malgré tout mon art: Monsieur de Santillane, me dit-il en souriant à la fin de mon récit, à ce que je vois, vous avez été tant soit peu *picaro*' (p. 387). The duc's assessment causes the reader to question Gil's character and the nature of his account. We have been won over to Gil's side because he is essentially a sympathetic victim of fortune rather than a malicious and clever rogue. Indeed, the minor characters in the tale tend to offer objective information about Gil's qualities. It is, at this late stage in the novel, that Lesage clarifies the issue for the reader by introducing Scipion as a valet for Gil. At the end of Scipion's own life story, Gil comments: 'Si dans son enfance Scipion était un vrai *Picaro,* il s'est depuis si bien corrigé qu'il est devenu le modèle d'un parfait domestique' (p. 535). Scipion is the internal comparison to Gil: he is unscrupulous in a way which Gil is not, stealing from the benevolent hermit, le frère Chrysostome, without conscience (p. 504). However, the point that Scipion makes, and it is important in our judgement of Gil, is that 'un fripon peut fort bien devenir un honnête homme' (p. 505). The same statement holds true for Gil.

At the beginning of the novel the reader is encouraged to expect rather a different kind of novel from the one he eventually gets. Gil's departure from home is accompanied by a theft. The parents' words of wisdom and advice, not to take the goods of others, are seen to be disregarded (p. 24). We learn, almost immediately, that Gil has stolen money from his uncle (p. 25). The prospects are not good. But as the novel proceeds so we realise that Gil is not the 'maître de mes actions' (p. 25) he claimed he was. Indeed, an important irony of the novel is that Gil's account of his life is eventually an account of how life has treated him. Never, at any stage in the novel, can the reader assume that Gil has found a stable situation. His role in the novel is not that of the crafty *picaro,* manœuvring with subtlety from master to master. He is one of life's victims – such indeed is the fate of the servant; his solution, eventually, is retirement from public life, away from the capriciousness of arbitrary power. What is apparent to the reader, and not to Gil, is that he never controls his own destiny. This, surely, is another of the ironies of the novel and one which Lesage examines throughout the text.

If we can assume that Lesage is using the idea of the picaresque novel to encourage a particular response from the reader then we can view the text more easily as a self-conscious fiction, where the author is making statements through the characters; the hero himself is unaware of the nature of these statements. More simply, what Lesage is doing in his flirtation with the picaresque is eliciting a constant critical response from the reader, one which will lead him to see Gil not as hero but as anti-hero. It is through this medium that Lesage's view of the world becomes apparent. The novel functions with a constant irony. Gil is not what he thinks he is: he is modified by events and he is never in control; the Spanish setting of the picaresque is a consequence of that irony. The reader – and even more especially the contemporary reader – is constantly aware of the unreality of the setting. If Lesage avoids 'realism' in his descriptions of Spain it is because his only concern is to describe a reality which is recognisably French. Lesage enters a complex game where he creates an illusion of Spain by using Spanish names, Spanish localities, Spanish customs and Spanish characters, but where it is always obvious that Spain is actually France and the fictional characters are, probably on more occasions than we realise, real characters. Surely here is the inherent meaning of the novel: the inability of characters to distinguish appearance from reality (which I shall discuss at length later) is simply a parallel to the reader's experience; if we strip the Spanish façade we find a coherent view of France. Lesage, through a naïve and uncomprehending figure like Gil, has introduced the ideal spectator: his mobility, his change of status and his lucidity, especially with regard to others, is the ideal tool for satire. Critics who analyse the novel at length with a view to defining it in terms of the picaresque are doing Lesage a great disservice. His use of the picaresque form is, in my interpretation, an ironical one and one which he tries hard to point out to the reader.

There is, as I have noted, a significant lack of physical, geographical detail. The journey through Spain (and beyond) allows Gil to change his social status and to meet new characters. It sometimes bothers critics that Lesage should write about Spain, even though he had never been there. All he needed was a map with place-names clearly indicated. The customs of Spain are those which are traditionally known: the use of chaperons and the characteristics of having a strong sense of honour and of vengeance are not ones which would necessitate a trip across the border to know about. Indeed, the lack of precision in detail should make us more aware of Lesage's real intentions. As Jacques Proust has pointed out (see *17*), Lesage does not avoid description as such but only what he terms 'romanesque' description and which may seem to be gratuitous in fiction. Indeed, description in a first-person account tells us more about the ability of the character to see for himself. The fact that there is little observation of the outside world must suggest to us that the character never succeeds in transcending himself and observing the world, except in so far as it affects him. As if to underline this point, Lesage, in the story told by don Raphaël which occupies practically the whole of Book V, shows don Raphaël to be singularly more 'aware' of the nature of his account than Gil Blas ever is. He states:

> J'aurais dans cet endroit de mon récit une occasion de vous faire une belle description de tempête, de peindre l'air tout en feu, de faire gronder la foudre, siffler les vents, soulever les flots, *et cœtera*. [*sic*] Mais laissant à part toutes ces fleurs de rhétorique, je vous dirai que l'orage fut violent et nous obligea de relâcher à la pointe de l'île de la Cabrera. (p. 263)

It is important that the reader should not take the illusion of Spain *too* literally. Lesage sprinkles the text with Spanish names and Spanish references – for example, describing the servants of the Archbishop of Grenada, 'Je ne pouvais croire

qu'ils fussent Espagnols' (p. 327) and Navarro's description of
d'Olivarès, 'On le dit vindicatif, mais quel Espagnol ne l'est
pas?' (p. 547) – but these references are not significant. They
maintain the pretence of the illusion of Spain but never make
the reader really doubt that Spain is in fact France.

If it is difficult for us to accept the illusion of Spain it
must have been singularly more so for the eighteenth-century
reader who would have recognised the many allusions more
easily. It is not helpful to compare *Gil Blas* with examples of
the Spanish picaresque unless one can deduce the meaning of
the novel from the comparison. It seems to me that what
Lesage is doing is using the picaresque as part of the subter-
fuge. The picaresque is a Spanish form and the reality
described is ostensibly Spanish. In *Gil Blas* Lesage uses the
idea of the picaresque as a point of reference. *Gil Blas*
develops according to a tradition but as the novel proceeds so
the distance between the tradition and the text increases. The
irony of the text is that the character of Gil himself becomes
progressively less significant and our sympathy for him de-
creases. We care about the young adolescent thrown into a
world he cannot comprehend. But as he starts to be part of
that world our relationship with him changes. What Lesage is
saying about his character is that he is not a good judge of
himself, but he can tell us much about the characters he
meets. So our perspectives change as we read the novel and as
the illusion of Spain becomes more emphatically France, or
perhaps even universal. The use of 'authentic' historical
figures is not convincing in a fictional framework. If Gil Blas
is present, history is fiction; and it is this fiction which the
author is using to make statements about reality.

2

Structure I: the Significance of Minor Characters

UNITY

IT would be impossible, here, to give a full account of the structure of the novel, of the variations of style, of the novel's failings and its qualities. What the reader must do, however, is appreciate the extent to which Lesage was conscious of the demands of this complex form and attempt to understand how he coped with structural and aesthetic problems. Critics have talked of the unity of *Gil Blas* and have gone to extremes to show that even the most unlikely incident bears some relationship to the main plot. Dédéyan, for example, states confidently: 'les épisodes même éloignés du récit principal se fondent dans le mouvement, dans le grand récit à forme personnelle, dans l'unité psychologique du meneur du jeu et de l'annoncier' (*4*, I, p. 163), and, I suspect, makes unity the most important criterion of quality. I think it may be more helpful to consider that Lesage's awareness of structural demands became more apparent to him as the novel proceeded and as the end came in sight. The early books are almost chaotic in structure; this is not to say the novel is defective, but simply that there are qualities related to variety. In other words, the novel takes shape in stages, as the external demands on novel form clarify.

There are thematic similarities, repeated episodes, recurring characters and some unity of location – although Spain is a big place; but the essential unifying factor of the novel is, of course, Gil Blas himself. He is *always* present – sometimes only a passive listener – but the novel's structure is based on a retrospective, selective account of episodes of his life. It is a loose structure because, on occasions, the people Gil meets are more interesting than he is himself. Let us not forget either that many of the 'minor' characters who tell stories introduce 'borrowings' from sources other than Lesage's imagination. I think that if one can accept the idea of a kind of compendium of stories with a loose unifying theme, the novel's qualities are more apparent and more enjoyable. Lesage's skill lies in the ordering of his material and the selectivity of his sources. We might, now, accuse Lesage of plagiarism – but at least it is entertaining plagiarism with a strong element of originality!

One critic at least has suggested that Gil's progress through life represents a kind of social ascension: 'Il y a donc un sens rigoureux et un choix délibéré dans la succession des maîtres et modèles de Gil Blas' (5, p. 15). Huet suggests that Gil's progress is paralleled by his improving capacity to imitate those he serves. Certainly Lesage pushes Gil forward, but the most interesting moments are related to the temporary falls from grace. The novel works on a constant irony which the reader is encouraged to pick up: Gil's fortune is simply a matter of chance. He has *certain* qualities, but so do others. Yet Gil prospers and others falter. Gil's strength, eventually, is that he recognises his luck and withdraws.

Roger Laufer defines 'unity' with a certain flexibility: there are unifying factors, money being the most obvious. He claims that 'money' is the most quoted 'object' in the novel (7, p. 293). But I suspect, without having made a count, that the most mentioned word is the first person pronoun, *Je,* and that this provides the essential unifying factor in the novel. Gil gives the disparate episodes a framework by including them in his retrospective account. Money is certainly an important factor in the novel because it allows the reader to make objective comparisons of a hierarchical nature. But the meaning of the novel is related to the fact that Gil eventually realises that money is only a means to an end: it is not a criterion of value. Gil did not fully understand the sense of the alchemist's words, but the reader is bound to bear them in mind. The alchemist's ability to change base metal into gold has brought him misery and anguish: 'Les richesses ne sont-elles pas un vrai supplice pour les personnes qui n'en jouis-

sent pas tranquillement?' (p. 351). Only after the disgrace of
d'Olivarès at the end of the novel is Gil able to understand
the nature of true happiness.

I shall concentrate later on the character of Gil and
analyse the changing states as time proceeds. For the moment, in order better to understand the structure of the novel,
I want to consider the role of the minor characters and the
contribution they make to the meaning of the text. Many
of the minor characters exist simply to give a breadth of
vision. A number of critics have suggested that *Gil Blas* is
a realistic novel because it contains so many characters of
different states. But realism is not a question of variety,
nor is it a matter of including 'low' characters for the sake
of balance. If we are to consider *Gil Blas* as a realistic
novel we must expect to be convinced by the illusion of
reality which is portrayed. This is simply not the case. We
are not convinced of the reality of Lesage's Spain, nor do we
ever really suspect that any of the characters actually existed
in the way we are told they did. Perhaps it is more precise to
suggest that a comic novel is working in a different way from
the sentimental or tragic novel. The constant ironical pattern
of a character observing himself introduces questions of a
different order. We find ourselves laughing at those episodes
in which the narrator is made to look ridiculous. But we
laugh even more when the narrator makes us laugh at him
unintentionally. Entertainment, at the expense of individuals
and groups, is the essential factor here. We will accept the
illusion of reality *only* if the entertainment value of the novel
is sufficiently great.

The minor characters who reappear are significant in this
interpretation, since it is through them that we are able to
judge the changing status of the narrator: Don Raphaël and
Ambroise are particularly important, as too are Laure and
Fabrice. Indeed, Lesage realised how crucial these characters
were by including them at key moments in Gil's life and by
structuring them into his denouement.

Gil Blas, at the end of his social ascension, looking back
over the different stages of his life, has to attempt to provide
an objective account of himself. He also has to try to describe

incidents and his reaction to them without making the knowledge of hindsight too obvious. Much of the comedy in the
novel derives from the tension which exists between the two
characters – Gil Blas, naïve and innocent, and Gil Blas, experienced and aware. Our enjoyment of the comic situations
which the young Gil Blas confronts will depend on the
author's ability to provide us with sufficient clues so that we,
at least, are not duped in the way Gil was. The most
important of the minor characters are able to provide constantly updated assessments of Gil's reality.

MINOR CHARACTERS

Don Raphaël appears first at Valladolid on the occasion
of a preposterous confidence trick. Camille, in league with
Ambroise and don Raphaël, described by Gil as 'plus belle
que jeune' (p. 67), claims to be a cousin of doña Mencia
whom Gil had assisted in escaping from the underground
hideout. Gil remembers the occasion at Peñaflor when he
had been tricked by a 'parasite'; the reader is clearly alerted
to the likelihood of a similar incident, yet Gil falls headlong
into the trap. Camille has his case put into her coach and Gil
is to be whisked away to her house: 'Elle prit soin elle-même
de faire mettre ma valise dedans, parce qu'il y avait, disait-
elle, bien des fripons à Valladolid. Ce qui n'était que trop
véritable' (p. 68). The retrospective comment added by Gil
sets the tone for the entire episode. When don Raphaël
arrives he is somehow too exuberant in his delight; the winks
and glances given by Camille to Gil are misinterpreted by
him but have a precise message for us. Suddenly the exchange
of rings takes place and the episode slots into place. Camille
leaves the room and next morning Gil awakes to find himself
alone and his money stolen: his faithful servant, Ambroise,
has gone too; retrospectively, Gil can now call him an
'hypocrite' (p. 70). The conclusion of the episode is significant: 'Au lieu de n'imputer qu'à moi ce triste incident, et de
songer qu'il ne me serait point arrivé si je n'eusse pas eu
l'indiscrétion de m'ouvrir à Majuelo sans nécessité, je m'en

pris à la fortune innocente et maudis cent fois mon étoile' (p.
71). Gil had been duped, but he is not yet able to understand
fully the error of his ways. The reader sees more clearly than
the character that Gil has not yet attained the maturity with
which to confront inveterate hoaxers like don Raphaël and
Ambroise.

When don Raphaël and Ambroise next appear they are
disguised as saintly hermits. The reader is surprised, as Gil
was, although a clue *is* in the text. When Gil first meets the
hermit we read: 'Venez, mes enfants, répondit l'anachorète
après m'avoir regardé avec attention' (p. 233). But the clue is
not sufficiently highlighted for us to understand the meaning.
The chance meeting with don Raphaël leads, not unnaturally, to his life story; indeed, the story takes up most of Book V
and diverts our attention away from Gil. Don Raphaël's story
shows the reader the differences between an innocent like Gil
Blas and a 'pícaro' like himself. Don Raphaël sins with pride;
he is uncommonly inventive, a master of disguise, and the
reader finds himself being amused by stories of deceit and
treachery. Don Raphaël is brave – he defends Moyadas with
courageous alacrity – but wicked. He steals from the two boys
who offer him hospitality, leaving them nothing: he is not at
all bothered about the predicament in which he leaves them
(p. 251). When Gil Blas, don Alphonse and the two rogues,
don Raphaël and Ambroise, conspire to defraud the Jew,
Samuel Simon, both don Alphonse and Gil express their
sense of guilt. The end of the first *livraison* is in sight and Gil
Blas has found himself a respectable master. The novel could
have ended there; and, in a sense, it did.

Don Raphaël and Ambroise do not appear in Books VII,
VIII or IX, so it is with considerable surprise that the reader
rediscovers them some twenty years later in the final *livraison*. They have now, apparently, learnt the error of their
ways and have become converted to Christianity. Both are
now monks and, as far as Gil can see, are sincere converts.
Yet the reader is not totally convinced, nor, significantly, is
don Alphonse: 'Monsieur le commissaire de l'Inquisition et
son greffier, dit-il, m'ont bien la mine de jouer ici une
nouvelle comédie' (p. 489). The doubt remains, and when the

two make off with the money from the monastery the reader is less surprised than Gil. Eventually, divine justice intervenes and the two rogues are executed by the Inquisition. Gil Blas points out to us that his fate might not have been dissimilar: the moral tone of the novel is guaranteed and the reader is left to ponder on the difference between two characters, don Raphaël and Gil Blas, whose paths had often crossed but whose destinies were quite different.

The structural roles of don Raphaël and Ambroise (and indeed of don Alphonse) are evident: the author introduces myriad characters in the novel, some of whom never reappear. But the reader cannot know, in advance, which of the characters will play recurring roles and the novelist plays with the reader's memory and imposes a structural order on him. The reader is bound to turn back the pages to remind himself of past events and in the course of doing so understands more easily the global vision of the author.

Laure too plays an important role in the novel, appearing, as she does, in Books III, VII and XII, in other words in each of the *livraisons*. She changes from servant to actress in the course of the novel and highlights, in the progression, the changes which occur to Gil himself. But even more important is the role played by Fabrice. For Gil Blas and Fabrice have a number of common characteristics and conditions. The first meeting, a surprise one, is crucial. Fabrice has accepted a modest position in life and shares none of the extravagant ambitions of Gil. The two were at school together and came from the same village. Fabrice is now happy, in service: 'Je ne finirais point, mon enfant, poursuivit-il, si je voulais dire tous les avantages des valets. Crois-moi, Gil Blas, perds pour jamais l'envie d'être précepteur, et suis mon exemple' (pp. 74-75). It is thanks to Fabrice that Gil finds his first position, with the *licencié* Sedillo, and that the progression from master to master begins. It would be convenient, but wrong, to say that the movement from master to master provides a consistent structural order for the novel. The diversity of Gil's masters and mistresses provides the expansive vision of reality and introduces a considerable amount of social satire. But it would be misleading to suggest that the structure of the novel is based simply on the changing status of Gil's employers.

It is Fabrice, more than any other minor character, who provides a kind of structural order: don Raphaël serves to highlight Gil's awareness and perception of the world, but it is Fabrice who provides the objective analysis of condition. Gil refers to him as 'mon cher Pylade' (p. 101) and not without good reason. Like Pylades, the friend of Orestes, characters who were both familiar to French readers through Racine's *Andromaque,* Fabrice is faithful and compassionate and his qualities are recognised by Gil. The role of Fabrice is enhanced by Lesage in the final books of the novel, as his condition changes from servant to writer. It is Fabrice's 'logement' which provides the most significant description of the entire novel (p. 363), and Fabrice's similarities with Gil provide the most consistent and meaningful comparison. It is Fabrice who offers the most important descriptions of Gil. His intimacy gives him a right that others do not share. As Gil was corrupted by life at court, so Fabrice pointed out to him: 'Avant que tu fusses à la Cour, tu avais toujours l'esprit tranquille. A présent je te vois sans cesse agité. [...] tu t'enveloppes et me caches le fond de ton âme. Je remarque même de la contrainte dans les honnêtetés que tu me fais' (p. 425). Gil, not surprisingly, does not accept Fabrice's observations: 'Je n'aperçois en moi aucun changement' (p. 425), he says. All the more need, therefore, for a character like Fabrice to point the changes out to the reader. The two friends argue and separate, only to be brought together again as the novel moves towards a conclusion. In the meantime, both have learned about the vicissitudes of fortune and are able to make the same assessment of life. Fabrice's apparent ease and wealth is stripped away by the bankruptcy of his patron, and the disgrace of d'Olivarès leads to Gil's retirement. Clearly, and not only for structural reasons, Fabrice's role in the novel is significant.

As Laufer has pointed out, the novel contains a vast quantity of minor characters, but there are some omissions in the overall perspective. We see little of the farming communities through which Gil passed and few merchants (7, p. 295).

What we do get in the minor characters is a good idea of the prejudices of the author. The view of reality which is represented is heavily inclined towards the Court, the medical profession and the theatre.

Minor characters who reappear are of a different order from those who appear only once. Not only do we pay more attention to incidents where there are recurring characters but we gain a greater sense of structure and control by comparing episodes and by referring back. The nature of the fiction is emphasised more especially by the coincidental reappearance of characters whom we have forgotten. One almost gets an impression of malicious delight on the part of Lesage as he delves back into the past and spirits out a forgotten character. Rolando, for example, the leader of the brigands, appears to have been left behind. Suddenly, in Madrid, Gil meets him again: 'Ma surprise fut extrême de le retrouver là, et je ne pus m'empêcher de frémir à sa vue' (p. 132). Of course his appearance can be seen to be related to the action, as Gil is given a choice of lifestyles. But the reader is amused at the coincidental meeting and shocked out of his complacency. As the coincidences are multiplied, so we realise that we are completely in the hands of the author. Moreover, the illusion which we have tacitly agreed to accept is threatened to breaking point by these almost frenetic rediscoveries. Indeed, the comic nature of the novel is related to this structural device, as the reader laughs at his own gullibility. As the characters reappear, so Gil Blas expresses his surprise (cf. pp. 93 (Camille), 102 (garçon-barbier), 179 (intendant de feu don Mathias), 223 (vieille femme de chambre de Constance), 321 (don Fernand de Leyva), 348 (Melchior Zapata), 469 (Manuel Ordoñez), 566 (don Gaston de Cogollos)). However fictional reality may be, the number of coincidences is simply too great – and I have not listed here the recurrence of don Alphonse, Fabrice or don Raphaël. Yet our enjoyment of the novel is not impaired by such unlikely events. On the contrary, it is enhanced. As Lesage clearly realises, the reader's amusement will depend, to a large extent, on his pleasure at observing himself being manipulated.

As he manipulated by the Archbishop.

Lesage is far more aware of the structural demands of the novel form than he is sometimes given credit for. Even without the recurring characters there are numerous deliberate references back which have the effect of drawing the threads of the novel together. Moreover, Lesage appears to be more conscious of these demands as the volumes proceed, and particularly in the second and third *livraisons*. So, for example, in Laure's story, she refers to an incident which relates to Gil: 'On me conduisit après cela dans une salle, où je trouvai un vieux moine, de je ne sais quel ordre, qui se mit à me prêcher la pénitence, à peu près comme la dame Léonarde t'exhorta dans le souterrain à la patience' (p. 338). The reference is as illustrative to us as it is to Gil. Similarly, when Gil Blas is asked to write a 'mémoire' for d'Olivarès he sets to work, 'après avoir invoqué le génie éloquent de l'archevêque de Grenade' (p. 552), recalling an important episode long since past (pp. 321-31). We see Lesage deliberately and methodically referring back to past incidents. When we talk of the unity of the novel a technique such as this is obviously crucial. It may appear artificial but this, perhaps more than anything else, is what gives the novel technical unity. (See also pp. 369/351 (the prediction), 381/332 (Navarro), 420/69 (the ring), 434/327 (don André de Tordesillas), 568/451 (don Gaston), 579/354 (Laure).)

It is tempting to conclude that Lesage's awareness of the demands of the novel form increased over the twenty or so years of composition. The apparent disorder of the structure of the novel with its unbalanced lengths of books and its sudden changes of emphasis is gradually catered for. Certainly, in the 1715 *livraison* we start to lose sight of the main character and the sub-plots begin to take over. Books V and VI contain little of Gil and much more of don Raphaël. When the novel started again in 1724 the author deliberately picked up the threads of the preceding chapter. It is not possible to read Books VII, VIII and IX, or X, XI and XII without, first, reading the 1715 volumes. In the 1715 volumes there were stories whose relationship to the main text is, to say the least, tenuous. This is not the case for the 1724 and 1735 volumes. Indeed, on a second reading, it is almost painfully apparent that in the 1735 volume Lesage is carefully tying the threads of the novel together. Book X especially provides a deliberate retrospective following Gil Blas's imprisonment and his new outlook on life. Book XI opens with a striking and quite unexpected incident: Gil's marriage to Antonia and the birth of their son (p. 538) is a cause of great rejoicing. We have waited long enough for the hero to be involved in some kind of sentimental relationship. Suddenly the situation changes. Both mother and son die and Gil Blas is left stunned. Their deaths are described with simplicity and a minimum of emotional appeal: 'Que le lecteur conçoive, s'il est possible, la douleur dont je fus saisi!' (p. 538).

Gil Blas is now free from domestic attachments, and after the disgrace of the duc de Lerme and the death of the King, he is able, once again, to return to Court. He soon rises to a position of power again, showing, in the process, the corruption of the Court environment and the abuse of authority. The repetition underlines the fact that corruption is not simply a consequence of particular individuals. It is endemic in an environment of flattery and personal favour. Lesage seems to borrow more and more from historical sources as the novel moves towards its end and Gil's role changes from comic, ironic participant to detached and wise historian. His character is modified by the emotional loss of his wife and son. It is their deaths which define the different tones of the two Court episodes. Under the duc de Lerme, Gil Blas is still avid for success, greedy in his acquisition of power and money. Under d'Olivarès he is older and wiser. He knows the fragility of his position and his confidence is constantly threatened.

By the fourth volume, of the 1735 *livraison,* the reader senses the conclusion. Gil Blas has retired from society and a process of retrospection begins as he retraces his footsteps, seeing Dr Sangrado in Valladolid and, by chance, Manuel Ordoñez. Death becomes the prominent feature as first his father (p. 472) then Séphora (p. 482), Julie (p. 498), his mother and his uncle (p. 557) and of course his wife and son (p. 538) are all accounted for. We sense a desire to satisfy our curiosity on the part of the author as he surveys the characters in the novel and fits them into their final resting places: don Alphonse (p. 565), Tordesillas (p. 571), don Gaston (p. 569). It is thanks to Gil's return to power and influence that don Alphonse and don André de Tordesillas can be amply rewarded. There is a final structural symmetry in the novel as we see Gil Blas returning 'home' to his castle at Lirias. Twenty-two years, we learn, have passed since his wife's death. It is time indeed for Gil Blas to settle down, and the final paragraph shows him leading a 'vie délicieuse', happily married (thanks to his 'lettres de noblesse', p. 607), the father of two children who will occupy his 'vieux jours'.

There is, obviously, a chronological unity to the novel as we trace Gil's journey through life. We lose sight of the precise details of the ageing process but it is a constant, forward process without retrospective interruption. The great difference, as I have said before, between the 1715 and the 1735 *livraisons* is that of narrative perspective. It is easier for Gil to laugh at himself as a silly, inexperienced youth, than it is to see himself with comic detachment as the time scale reduces. Only three years separate the writing process from the final incidents in the account. What Lesage has shown is that the progression of time and the acquisition of awareness gradually erode the comic possibilities.

3
Structure II:
The Interpolated Stories

SEVENTEENTH-CENTURY novels, as Vivienne Mylne has pointed out (*14*, pp. 57-61), often included interpolated *histoires*. The episodic structure of a novel allowed easy integration of such intercalated stories. Clearly, when writing *Gil Blas*, Lesage was using the tradition with the intention of diversification and amusement. We have to accept the convention whereby characters in the novel introduce their own accounts without seriously expecting all these tales to have the same vital relationship with the main story. Quite simply, some will be more relevant than others. Many modern readers find the interpolations obstructive and distracting. It is possible to respond by asserting that the intercalated stories provide an ingredient for success which is lacking in Gil's own narrative: they are, often, more interesting, more moving and more subtle than Gil's view of himself.

Lesage compensates for the failures in Gil's account by the inclusion of these *histoires*, he broadens the vision of the novel, increases its emotional complexity, and goes beyond the frontiers of Spain. Many of the stories are borrowed from other sources and are clearly identified in the Laufer edition. They should not, I think, be seen as parodies of other works. On the contrary, there is no real attempt to mock the original source.

The interpolated stories begin remarkably early in the novel: when Gil is captured by the brigands, such is the noise and confusion over dinner that Rolando, the captain, calls for silence and asks his fellow villains to tell their life-stories. Gil Blas is fortunate indeed that these stories have not been told before his arrival, but such are the conventions of the interpolated story: Rolando says, 'Il me vient une pensée. Depuis que nous sommes associés, nous n'avons pas eu la curiosité de nous demander quelles sont nos familles et par quel enchaînement d'aventures nous avons embrassé notre profession' (p. 35). The introduction of these short stories may be somewhat clumsy, but the pattern is set then and there for the entire novel. By the end of the chapter Gil Blas has been told about the nature of the world: 'tous les hommes aiment à s'approprier le bien d'autrui. C'est un sentiment général. La manière seule en est différente' (p. 39).

Obviously, Gil is bound to escape; it is inconceivable that the entire novel should take place in the restricted setting of an underground hideout. Lesage relates the escape to the story of doña Mencia de Mosquera (pp. 51-56, 62-63). Her story is of a quite different order from anything that has preceded it in the novel, being elevated and tragic and demanding an emotional response from the reader. It is told with concision and economy: the basic facts are sufficient to arouse the reader's compassion. Doña Mencia is presented with a problematic choice, between love and money. Her choice of the former, only to find it cruelly destroyed, introduces our response, and that of Gil: 'Je pleurai même aussi, tant il est naturel de s'intéresser pour les malheureux et particulièrement pour une belle personne affligée' (p. 56). Doña Mencia's tale raises the tone of the novel and introduces the first obviously dramatic incident. Moreover, it allows the emotional response of Gil Blas himself and situates his character. It is remarkably well integrated into the main story and is rendered all the more dramatic by the interruption to it, occasioned by Gil's arrest. Eventually, of course, it is the money and the ring which doña Mencia gives to Gil which lead to his being tricked by don Raphaël, Camille and Ambroise. It is both part of the main story and yet distinct from it. Following doña Mencia's tale, Gil is able to make a clear statement of his ambition: 'Je veux porter l'épée et tâcher de faire fortune dans le monde' (p. 64). It is tempting, indeed, to say that Gil is inspired by doña Mencia and that this chance meeting is the one which determines his future.

Other interpolated stories are less well integrated. The story of the 'garçon-barbier' (pp. 103-19) with its comic account of an abortive seduction and the hero being mistaken for a noisy cat is trivial but amusing; it serves to pass the time and to advance the journey. The story of don Pompeyo de Castro (pp. 156-62), overheard by Gil, is elevated in tone; it is not obviously related to Gil's story, but it introduces a general statement about the nature of life which the careful reader will no doubt bear in mind: 'les plaisirs de la vie ne sont pas d'éternelle durée' (p. 158).

It is not possible to make any general descriptive statement about the interpolated stories. Those told by characters who play a major role in Gil's story will obviously be those whose relationship to the main body of the text is most apparent. The stories of don Raphaël (pp. 250-95), Laure (pp. 338-47) and Scipion (pp. 500-35) are simply extensions of Gil's own story. Stylistically it is impossible to distinguish between these related first-person accounts. Other stories appear to emphasise the 'Spanish' nature of the novel with the emphasis on honour, passion and vengeance. (See especially don Roger de Rada, pp. 401-07), and don Gaston de Cogollos, pp. 439-51.) But the most striking of all the interpolated stories is Lesage's adaptation of a play by Francisco de Rojas y Zorrilla, *Casarse por vengarse*. Its link with Gil's story is accidental, to say the least. A striking painting in the castle of Elvire, which Gil sees while serving the beautiful Aurore, is the pretext for this 'nouvelle'. It is a third-person account of a tragic tale of love and vengeance, in which the King is obliged, through trickery, to marry against his will. It is of a quite different nature from the story of Gil Blas; indeed, it is even out of place. Yet it remains a remarkably fine tale and one whose message could be that appearances are not always reliable signs of reality. Enrique, the King, *appears* to have betrayed his oath to Blanche, but in fact Blanche's father misused a signed paper and, for the sake of the State, obliged Enrique to marry Constance. Blanche married another, a duel took place and her husband died, but not before killing her, and the King was left to survive in misery.

The story is a remarkably dramatic one which emphasises the lack of emotional drama in Gil's own story. It does have a

thematic link with the novel as a whole: but such a link
demands a very close reading and one which many readers
will simply not perceive, especially at a first approach. In
other words, the view that appearances do not coincide with
reality is *one* interpretation which could be given to the
Mariage de vengeance. But is this interpretation sufficiently
clear to justify its presence? It would certainly be possible to
omit the *Mariage de vengeance* and still to enjoy and understand *Gil Blas*. But it is also possible that one's enjoyment is
enhanced by reading the short extra. It is worth pointing out
too that the *Mariage de vengeance* does have a thematic
similarity with another interpolated story more closely con-
nected with Gil's account, that of don Gaston de Cogollos,
the story which relates the rivalry of two men for the hand of
doña Helena, the duel, the enforced departure and, eventually, marriage to a man who gained the girl's affection by
deception.

While there are some similarities between the stories there
are, clearly, many differences. However, what they have in
common – and this, surely, is their significance here, is that
they provide a dramatic, passionate, love element of a serious
and tragic nature which Gil Blas's account lacks. It is difficult
to take Gil Blas seriously when we know him as intimately as
we do: there is always the suspicion of comedy when he
becomes involved in amorous intrigues and always the expectation of ironic commentary. This is not the case for the
interpolated stories which we are willing to take at face value.
The interpolations have an important role in the novel:
sometimes they will confirm a view of reality suggested by
Gil's account; they will introduce similar elements of satire –
it is no coincidence that Laure becomes an actress having
served a 'comédienne', nor that Lucinde, the mother of don
Raphaël who eventually tells her story (pp. 273-78), was an
actress and has evidently left her mark on her son. His own
story begins, 'Je suis fils d'une comédienne de Madrid', and
his perception of reality and his ability to disguise and
defraud are clearly based on a particular appreciation of the
nature of the real world. As we shall see later, perhaps
the major theme of the novel, and the unifying thread of the

work, is that appearance does not always coincide with reality. The roles of don Raphaël and his mother and the role of the interpolated stories generally might best be appreciated in this context. But the most important feature of the interpolated stories is, surely, that by adding a further dimension to the novel they increase our enjoyment. Without them, *Gil Blas* would be bare indeed.

4

Novel Form: Qualities and Defects

QUALITIES

L E S A G E ' S novel is rarely given the technical credit which it is due, nor is it often appreciated that the author shows a remarkable awareness of the form he has chosen. First-person narratives make particular demands on the reader, who, accepting the illusion of a real person telling his life story, is bound to treat the account with suspicion. Does it reveal an element of self-glorification or justification? Is the narrator telling the whole truth? What is the relationship between author and narrator? To what extent is the irony of the account dependent on the tension between the two? Does the narrator's account include an unwitting element of self-criticism? Is the meaning of the novel and our assessment of reality strictly dependent on this element of self-criticism? Many novelists are not sufficiently aware of the form they have chosen to go beyond simple story-telling. Lesage, it seems to me, shows sufficient awareness of his medium for us to be justified in endowing the novel with extra meaning. This is not to say that the work is not without its defects and its awkward moments.

I think that Lesage's awareness of the form grows over the period of composition. The novel gives every indication of having been written in stages – like a building without a precise architectural plan built by an imaginative master-builder. Ideas came in writing and were incorporated gradually.

For the illusion of the reality to be maintained in a first-person account either it must be admitted that on occasions the individual was not aware of an event taking place in his absence, or some justification for external evidence must be given. If first-person narrators know and describe too much, their very reality is threatened.

Lesage is not always very subtle in coping with such difficulties, but at least he is aware of the problems. In order to hear don Pompeyo's story Gil Blas has to listen at the door: 'Au lieu de nous retirer, nous nous étions arrêtés à la porte, que nous avions laissée entr'ouverte, et de là nous n'en avions pas perdu un mot' (p. 162). Lesage overcomes the difficulty of presence but he simply follows the convention whereby people listening to stories remember them word for word and can write them down verbatim. In don Raphaël's story, in the account of his deception of Jérôme de Moyadas, we read: 'Dès le lendemain, une espèce de paysan, chargé d'une valise, arriva chez le père de Florentine. Je ne m'y trouvai point alors: mais mon camarade y était' (p. 256). Indeed, Moralés, the 'camarade' in question, plays a vital role in the account; without his presence the illusion of reality is shattered since don Raphaël cannot possibly explain what happens when he is not present. In the same interpolated story, don Raphaël describes his attempt to seduce Violante, the wife of don Baltazar. Don Raphaël, caught in a compromising situation, is obliged to make a quick get-away. He remarks: 'D'abord que j'eus disparu, les femmes, que l'arrivée imprévue de ce mari avait troublées, se rassurèrent, et le reçurent avec tant d'effronterie, qu'il se douta bien qu'on m'avait caché ou fait évader' (p. 289). How, the reader might ask, does don Raphaël know how the women reacted if he was not there? It is tempting to say that Lesage has realised the predicament. He, or rather don Raphaël, adds: 'Je ne vous dirai point ce qu'il dit à doña Inès et à sa femme. C'est une chose qui n'est pas venue à ma connaissance' (p. 289). The illusion is retrieved – but only just – and the reader is mocked in the process.

But the most striking example of this device, and one which adds an element of comedy to the anecdote, is Scipion's story of his part of King in the play presented for the Archbishop of Seville. Scipion leaves the stage and runs away in his magnificent dress, which he sells to a 'fripier'. Later, at an inn, he overhears the end of his story being told to entertain the company:

> Messieurs [...] je vous garde pour la bonne bouche une histoire des plus divertissantes, une aventure arrivée ces jours passés à l'archevêché de Séville. [...] Ce personnage en fit un récit fidèle, et m'apprit même ce que j'ignorais, c'est à dire ce qui s'était passé dans la salle après mon départ...   (p. 515)

The archbishop, we learn, took the conclusion of the play in good heart and introduced his own comic ending.

Lesage shows a constant awareness of the reader's presence and even invites his participation in the account. Gil's narrative is, unlike some *mémoires,* intended for the reading public. For example, when he starts to make a financial success of his role as secretary to the duc de Lerme, he anticipates the reader's response: 'Il me semble que j'entends un lecteur qui me crie en cet endroit: Courage, Monsieur de Santillane! mettez du foin dans vos bottes. Vous êtes en beau chemin. Poussez votre fortune' (p. 408). There is, clearly, a dialogue taking place between narrator and reader, and it is one in which the reader is encouraged to participate. Similarly, when in the service of the duc d'Olivarès, before relating the assistance he gave to don André de Tordesillas, Gil notes:

> J'eus bientôt encore une autre occasion d'employer mon crédit pour un ami; ce que je crois devoir rapporter, pour faire connaître à mes lecteurs que je n'étais plus ce même Gil Blas qui sous le ministère précédent vendait les grâces de la Cour.   (p. 566)

Not only is Gil interested in a dialogue but he is particularly keen to provoke a favourable response from his reader. The intimacy of the relationship between narrator and reader is one which Lesage encourages. We may laugh at Gil Blas but our laughter is not malicious. Malice is reserved for others and Gil needs us as his allies.

Our proximity to Gil and his inclination to portray himself as a comic character are the foundations of the relationship between narrator and reader. Gil's credibility is based on his willingness to see himself in an unfavourable light. The illusion of reality is strengthened by this willingness and by Gil's guarantees of the 'truth' of his account (see also pp. 351, 538, 580).

Lesage uses the conventional language of storytelling to give authority to Gil's narration: 'Il faut dire la vérité, je me servis de cette occasion pour donner de nouvelles larmes à la mémoire d'Antonia' (p. 559). But it is the triviality of many incidents which, paradoxically, guarantees the 'truth' of an account. When Gil and his fellow companions decide to rescue the man and woman captured by brigands (who turn out to be the comte de Polan and Séraphine), Gil admits, honestly, that the danger to his safety was not great (p. 296). This respect for truth allows the reader to accept the incredibility of certain other episodes with a little more ease. It seems highly unlikely that the comte de Polan and Séraphine should not be immediately recognised by Gil and by don Alphonse, but they were not, according to the 'true' description of the incident.

There is an awareness in the novel of the demands of an account of this nature, and Lesage introduces into the text a number of examples which quite specifically serve to analyse the text itself. We have, for example, characters commenting on others' stories, and even showing awareness of the style and length of their own accounts. After don Raphaël's story, which takes up such a large part of Book V, Gil begins the next chapter saying: 'Quand don Raphaël eut achevé de conter son histoire, dont le récit me parut un peu long, don Alphonse par politesse lui témoigna qu'elle l'avait fort diverti' (p. 295). Don Alphonse, we assume, is only being polite when he said how much he enjoyed it – or at least, that is Gil's interpretation based on his own assessment of don Raphaël's story. Our own reaction is likely to be more generous: we are at least as amused by don Raphaël's story as we are by Gil's, but Gil seems to be saying that time not spent on him is time wasted. A similar, perhaps more insensitive, remark is made by Gil when he listens to his mother's account of what has happened since he left home:

Elle me fit un ample détail des chagrins qu'elle avait essuyés
dans les maisons où elle avait été duègne, et me dit là-dessus
une infinité de choses que je n'aurais pas été bien aise que
mon secrétaire eût entendues, quoique je n'eusse rien de caché
pour lui. Avec tout le respect que je dois à la mémoire de ma
mère, la bonne dame était un peu prolixe dans ses récits; elle
m'aurait fait grâce de trois quarts de son histoire, si elle en eût
supprimé les circonstances inutiles.   (pp. 472-73)

Gil's response is harsh indeed and must reflect, to some
extent, on his character. His lack of tolerance at the length of
his mother's story (which we are not given in full) should, I
assume, encourage a corresponding awareness of the nature of
his own account. Are all the details that Gil tells us about
himself really so important? His comments on his mother's
story have the effect of inviting the reader's comments on his.
We may conclude that Gil himself is more sensitive about
other's stories than he is about his own.

Even so, Gil shows an awareness of style that is rarely
found in comic heroes of the day. The archbishop of Grenada
is sufficiently impressed by his style to employ him as
secretary (p. 323) as too are the duc de Lerme and the duc
d'Olivarès. The duc de Lerme informs him of the need for a
style which is both 'net' and 'concis' (p. 387) and Gil succeeds
in producing the required tone. D'Olivarès remarks: 'Je ne
m'étonne plus si le duc de Lerme exerçait ta plume. Ton style
est concis et même élégant; mais je le trouve un peu trop
naturel' (pp. 549-50). Are we to accept these internal criticisms of Gil's style as correct? Or must they also be seen in
the perspective of the first-person narrative where everything,
even comments by others, are really comments by the self
about the self? Whatever we decide, we can, nevertheless,
conclude that Lesage is constantly aware of the nature of
fiction, and that he attempted to encourage aesthetic debate
by the use of what might now be called self-conscious
narration. Gil Blas is both narrator and narratee in the
account: this double perspective allows him to comment on
others' stories while, at the same time, inviting comment on
his own. The criticisms he makes of others must be levelled

at him; the true dialogue, clearly, is not the one between Gil Blas and the reader but the one between Lesage and us.

The fact that Gil is *aware* poses particular problems of interpretation of character. Confessions, as Rousseau was later to realise, have a defensive and justificatory purpose. Gil is able to observe himself telling others details of his life but forgets, on occasions, that his confessions then will not be forgotten in our own assessment of him. So, for example, when he wishes to enter the household of the duc de Lerme, he realises that if he gives an authentic, true account of himself, the duc de Lerme will be unlikely to employ him:

> Il exigea même de moi là-dessus une narration sincère. Quel détail c'était me demander! De mentir, devant un premier ministre d'Espagne, il n'y avait pas d'apparence. D'une autre part, j'avais tant de choses à dire aux dépens de ma vanité, que je ne pouvais me résoudre à une confession générale. Comment sortir de cet embarras? Je pris le parti de farder la vérité dans les endroits où elle aurait fait peur toute nue. (pp. 386-87)

He meets the same predicament with the duc d'Olivarès and decides on the same solution: '[je] passai légèrement sur les choses qui me faisaient peu d'honneur' (p. 546). What is the reader to make of these admissions? Gil has said that he is telling us the truth. But does he know what the truth is, and is he not inviting suspicion by showing himself, on occasions, to be deliberately deceitful?

As Lesage clearly realises, first-person narratives introduce complex problems of authenticity that third-person, historical forms quite simply evade. It is my contention that in *Gil Blas* Lesage is encouraging an aesthetic debate and an analysis of the first-person narrative form. As I shall reassert later, the one consistent theme or 'meaning' of the novel is that appearance does not always coincide with reality: Gil himself progresses through life hoping to attain the knowledge and awareness he needs to make the distinctions with clarity; his failure to do so is paralleled by the failure of his own account. He does not convince us fully that he ever is what he appears to be and what he claims he is. The essential irony of the text is that we remain external and critical towards Gil Blas, even on those occasions when he thinks he is closest to us.

DEFECTS

But there is also a further problem of attribution: in a novel which is self-aware do we attribute defects to the narrator or to the author? It is tempting to say to the former, but to do so would be to give Lesage too much credit. There are a number of defects in the novel which cannot be seen as 'ironical' defects; they do not cast any light on our interpretation of Gil's character. One obvious failure, clearly pointed out by Mylne (*14,* p. 56) is the inability of the narrator to explain differences of styles: others' stories should, in reality, be similar in style to Gil's own story since it is *he* who is telling them. But they are not, and the inconsistency is not catered for.

Lesage fails to assimilate all of the borrowings he makes into the main text. This is particularly apparent at the end of the novel as he relies more and more on Siri for his descriptions of a historical nature (see especially p. 547).

There are an excessive number of characters in the novel with similar names. Our problem, and this may well be explained by the long period of composition, is that we find it impossible, especially on a first reading, to identify those characters who will reappear and even become important. Lesage could have introduced a few more clues to guide the reader through the maze. Similarly, the use of different names to describe the same character is bound to confuse the reader. Lesage could have used 'Ambroise' or 'Lamela' consistently, but not both; the 'intendant de don Mathias' or 'Gregorio Rodriguez'. For simplicity's sake the reader must be given help with identification. A further difficulty, and this might well be explained by the ambiguous nature of the text, is the use, almost indiscriminately, of French and Spanish versions of the same name. Kimena/Chimène (pp. 216-17), doña Eufrasia/Eufrasie (pp. 222/223), Margarita/Marguerite

(p. 587). The reader expects consistency and is annoyed by the lack of it.

As the years go by and the characters reappear, so the inventive capacity of the author appears to decline and the rediscovery of past figures appears to be almost gratuitous: for example, the reunion with Fabrice is introduced: 'Un jour, en revenant de l'un de ces endroits, je passai devant la porte d'un hôpital. Il me prit envie d'y entrer' (p. 553). There are, increasingly in Books VII-XII, difficult, clumsy moments of transition:

> Il y a longtemps que je n'ai parlé du comte de Lemos. Venons présentement à ce seigneur.   (p. 414)

> Laissons là mon mariage pour un moment. L'ordre de mon histoire le demande, et veut que je raconte le service que je rendis à don Alphonse, mon ancien maître.   (p. 430)

As one reads the novel one is conscious, at the same time, of a growing awareness of the demands and subtleties of the novel form and yet a diminution in the inventive power of the imagination. Certain incidents appear to be dull repetitions of previous ones (the 'fripier' episodes, pp. 64-65 and 513-14), and there is at least one clumsy repetition of information which indicates careless composition (see p. 588, the references to don Henri-Philippe de Guzman).

Many of the faults are attributable to the problems of writing a novel with sequels – it simply was not obvious in 1715 what was going to happen in 1735 and we are demanding readers since we expect a uniform text. But the novel very evidently has more qualities than defects, and many of these qualities counteract the precise deficiencies I have enumerated.

Lesage's greatest quality in *Gil Blas* is, of course, his ability to perceive the comic nature of life. It is particularly in his descriptions of character that such a quality emerges, and in those short extracts which we can define as 'portraits' at which Lesage excels. The description given of Carlos Alonso de la Ventoleria (the actor/author Baron in real life) by Laure is a masterpiece of satirical observation (pp. 171-72).

So too is the portrait of don Annibal (pp. 356-57) and many others besides. As we shall see, the qualities of Lesage's novel are essentially those which can be defined by his comic vision. It is to the comedy of the novel, in its diverse forms, that we must now turn our attention.

5

A Comic Novel

I f Lesage's novel can still be read with pleasure today it is essentially because of the author's comic vision. Lesage managed to produce a work which is both general and specific in its comedy, treating both types and individuals, dealing with what is comic in reality and producing imagined scenes of wit and insight. The ironical position of the narrator is one obvious source of comedy: we laugh at Gil when he expects us to, but we also laugh when he expects it least. Lesage sees that the world is intrinsically comic: people take themselves too seriously and appear not to understand that others see them as part of the human comedy. Lesage's vision of humanity leads, naturally, to satire – of types, institutions and of real characters. At the same time the narrator's perception of reality will introduce comedy which is part of the observation of the real world. Comedy represents the unifying tone of the novel; it is not surprising that, in a comic novel, even the serious and tragic tend towards comedy, since the reader is expecting a sudden surprise or trick on every occasion. It is hard to take the serious seriously.

S a t i r e :

(i) *Medicine*

The most obvious element of comedy in the novel is that which satirises the medical profession. There is a clear debt to Molière in the presentation of characters who ask fortunes to kill off their patients. Sangrado plays the largest part in this satire; the language Gil uses to describe his activities is extravagant and indicative: 'Ce savant médecin avait l'extérieur grave. Il pesait ses discours et donnait de la noblesse à ses expressions. Ses raisonnements paraissaient géométriques, et ses opinions fort singulières' (p. 82). The reader smells a rat! We sense hypocrisy, deceit and trickery, but Gil, at the moment of the experience, appeared less aware of the reality than he does now, in retrospect. Clearly we laugh at Sangrado but we also laugh at Gil.

Sangrado's pompous pronouncements on the nature of the human being make us, as readers, immediately suspicious: 'C'est une erreur de penser que le sang soit nécessaire à la conservation de la vie. On ne peut trop saigner un malade' (p. 82). His medical philosophy is to drain the body of all its blood and to replace the blood by water. Not surprisingly, his success rate is low, and Gil soon realises the nature of the universal panacea and appreciates that with such a simple philosophy he too can become a doctor and, eventually, earn a fortune. Which is what he intends to do, at least until his life is threatened and he abandons his promising medical career. Now, later, Gil appreciates the inefficacy of Sangrado's cures. At the time, however, he was not able to perceive the reality which is only too clear to us: 'Comme je n'étais qu'un jeune médecin qui n'avait pas encore eu le temps de s'endurcir au meurtre, je m'affligeais des événements funestes qu'on pouvait m'imputer' (p. 99). The double perspective of Gil then/Gil now heightens the comedy for the reader. We care little for the unfortunate patients who are expedited to an early grave. They are purely functional beings who have no place in our range of sentiments. But Gil, to his credit, expresses some concern.

If Sangrado were the only doctor involved in this satire we might conclude that Lesage is simply trying to introduce a scene which is intrinsically comic. But he goes one stage further. When Gil, much later, retraces his footsteps, he returns via Valladolid and finds Sangrado drinking wine, something which he had expressly forbidden. Sangrado knows he is caught out, but manages a comic response; he has found the perfect compromise: he dilutes his wine with water ('mon vin est bien trempé', p. 469).

On practically every occasion in the novel when Gil or anyone has recourse to a doctor we find a brief, critical remark decrying the 'profession'. So, for example, when don Alphonse is struck down by a fever which threatens his life, he survives because there were no doctors available (p. 308). When Gil is unconscious and treated, at great expense, by doctors he remarks, on recovery: 'je maudissais jusqu'aux universités où ces messieurs reçoivent le pouvoir de tuer les hommes impunément' (p. 377). There are similar, critical, remarks throughout the novel: pp. 180, 186, 224, 379-80, 455-56, 528, 534, and finally p. 601, when three doctors combine to kill off d'Olivarès and bring the novel to a conclusion. On one occasion only, in the story of don Gaston, can the medical profession be praised for its efficiency: 'Tout dangereusement blessé que j'étais, l'habileté des chirurgiens me tira bientôt d'affaire' (p. 443). Surgeons are not doctors, however, and cannot redress the balance of the novel as a whole. Lesage's repetition of the theme is, eventually, as comic as the theme itself. The reader comes to expect a critical remark in every appearance of a doctor, and he is seldom disappointed.

(ii) *The Church*

Such comedy can be described as traditional: it is not simply comic because of the nature of the profession but because behind the façade of a doctor we see a hypocrite. Much the same kind of analysis can be made for the clergy and the judiciary as they appear in the novel. Gil's uncle, a cleric, learns to read his breviary correctly for the first time while he is teaching Gil to read. The archbishopric of Grenada houses both 'vrais' and 'faux dévots', as Melchior de la Ronda points out to Gil (p. 324). And in Laure's story, in her description of Pedro Zendono, the steward of the hôpital de la Pitié, she remarks to Gil: 'Tu n'as jamais vu de face si hypocrite, quoique tu aies demeuré à l'archevêché' (p. 339). But the clergy are not important figures of satire. Lesage, like Marivaux in *Le Paysan parvenu,* was more interested in highlighting recognisable 'faux dévots' than in attacking the church or its beliefs.

(iii) *Justice*

The criticism of the judiciary in the novel is levelled more at the agents of the law than at the laws themselves or the judges who interpret them. Indeed, the satire here is comic only in that we see Gil becoming an innocent victim of forces greater than himself on occasions when he felt he had escaped. He is searched after his wrongful arrest when accompanying doña Mencia: 'ils vidèrent tout doucement mes poches et me prirent ce que les voleurs même avaient respecté, je veux dire les quarante ducats de mon oncle' (p. 57). When he is released from prison he remarks: 'Je ne me plains pas de la justice [...] Elle est très équitable. Je voudrais seulement que tous ses officiers fussent d'honnêtes gens' (p. 60). This satire of justice and the references we find elsewhere (pp. 94, 98-99, 286) tell us more about Gil's perception of human nature than justice itself. As Gil ages, so he realises that men are basically very similar: they wear different disguises but these appearances do not mask their real characters. The comedy of this form of satire is directed as much at Gil himself as it is at the apparent object of satire.

Gil's *naïveté* means that he is unaware of the corruption of the world and can fully understand it only when he is part of it. His changing status broadens his vision and introduces a vast range of satire.

(iv) *The State*

As secretary to the duc de Lerme, and, to a lesser extent, when he is secretary to d'Olivarès, Gil realises the power he can exert. He sells favours and soon amasses great wealth. Such rises to fortune were not unknown in the Regency. What Gil does not appear to understand, however, is that he is attempting, in his rise to power, to resemble those people he has served and despised. In satirising others, he is also satirising himself. Only after his imprisonment and disgrace is Gil lucid enough to state the lesson he has learnt: 'Les biens ne sont propres qu'à corrompre mes mœurs. [...] Les richesses sont un fardeau dans une retraite où l'on ne cherche que la tranquillité' (p. 461). Of course the state is not excluded from the satirical intentions of the author. But his real skill lies in his ability to satirise both hero and others simultaneously.

(v) *'Littérateurs'*

Lesage is at his best and most critical when satirising those elements of society he knew best: the world of literature and the world of the theatre. It is mainly through the character of Fabrice that Lesage introduces his presentation of the literary scene which allows a clear statement of his own prejudices and beliefs. There appears to be a constant, unifying theme that there is no reliable guide to literary quality: fashion, taste, self-interest and conceit all play a part in defining success, but, according to Lesage, quality and success should not necessarily be equated.

In the description of the salon of the marquise de Chaves (assumed to be the real-life marquise de Lambert (1647-1733) who was well known for her twice-weekly salon) Gil notices a disparity between the taste of the *habitués* and the general public. Comedy was generally despised:

> On n'y regardait la meilleure comédie ou le roman le plus ingénieux et le plus égayé que comme une faible production qui ne méritait aucune louange; au lieu que le moindre ouvrage sérieux, une ode, une églogue, un sonnet y passait pour le plus grand effort de l'esprit humain. Il arrivait souvent que le public ne confirmait pas les jugements du bureau, et que même il sifflait quelquefois impoliment les pièces qu'on y avait fort applaudies. (p. 228)

One gets a very clear impression of satire here, of people, readers and critics, whose taste is based on prejudice rather than quality, to the detriment of comic authors like Lesage himself. The adverb 'impoliment' is crucial in this remark, suggesting, ironically, impudence on the part of the general public which has the cheek to disagree with the opinion of the few.

The consistent belief which Lesage appears to be putting
forward is that good works will be harshly criticised while
mediocrity will slip through unnoticed. So, for example, in
don Raphaël's story, he explains how he became a poet: 'Je
m'érigeai même en poète et je consacrai ma muse aux
louanges du prince. Je demeure d'accord de bonne foi que
mes vers n'étaient pas bons. Aussi ne furent-ils pas critiqués'
(p. 281). Lesage is trying to state what appears to be a
paradox which works to the detriment of quality and to the
advantage of mediocrity. We can see that *Gil Blas* represents
not only a comic vision of the world but a specific attack on
certain prejudices and beliefs. It becomes a mouthpiece for
Lesage himself. We are a far cry from the picaresque novel
and much closer to a comic *roman de mœurs*.

When Gil meets Fabrice at court having lost sight of him
after leaving Valladolid in a hurry, he is not told immediately
of the important change which has taken place. Fabrice's new
lot in life appears to be a happy one. His 'appartement' is, in
fact, a room divided into four, reached by a dark and narrow
staircase and decorated with maps and old theses. The bed is
old and worn and the rest of the furniture is showing clear
signs of age. We are kept in the same suspense as Gil. Fabrice
appears to be happy, apparently unaware of the reality which
surrounds him, yet which is perceived by Gil and which
represents the only indicative descriptive reality of the novel.
Finally, Fabrice announces his new occupation: he is an
author! Moreover, he says, modestly(!), he is a good author.
Gil is, not unnaturally, surprised at Fabrice's new condition.
Fabrice soon explains how he came to write: he wrote a play
which, on his own admission, was worth nothing but which
was a great success. He concluded: 'Je jugeai par là que le
public était une bonne vache à lait qui se laissait aisément
traire' (p. 364). And so begins an important literary debate.
Fabrice, like other authors, has an elevated view of himself.
Gil is detached and ironic in his remarks and is allowed to
comment on one of Fabrice's sonnets (one remembers Alceste's
remarks on Oronte in Molière's *Le Misanthrope*). Gil
finds the poem obscure and incomprehensible, to which
Fabrice responds: 'tant mieux! Les sonnets, les odes et les

autres ouvrages qui veulent du sublime ne s'accommodent
pas du simple et du naturel. C'est l'obscurité qui en fait tout
le mérite' (p. 365). Gil disagrees, of course, but Lesage has
made his point. If the public is unable to distinguish between
quality and worthlessness, it deserves all the bad authors who
supply its needs. As we read the novel we get an ever growing
impression that what Lesage is saying is that literary success
is not a guarantee of literary quality. Other factors are at play:
the literary world is a refined version of the real world where
hypocrisy and pomposity are constant features.

When Gil dines with a number of poets brought by
Fabrice he is led to the conclusion that 'la nation des auteurs
est un peu vaine et glorieuse' (p. 412). Fabrice is no exception
to this general rule, nor indeed are other writers as they are
presented in the novel: the archevêque de Grenade (pp. 321-31),
Gabriel Triaquero (pp. 483-85), don Ignacio de Ipigna
(p. 533) and, of course, Gil himself, who is quite conscious
of the excellent quality of his prose! ('J'étais devenu une
espèce d'auteur', p. 358, and on page 550, his style is
remarked upon by d'Olivarès.)

The world of literature is a world of hypocrisy and petty
jealousy, a world of rivalry and antagonisms where literary
quality appears unimportant. One senses an expression of
Lesage's own views of the unjust treatment he felt he had
received at the hands of critics. Fabrice, from this point of
view, is an ideal character. He plays the part of a poet to
perfection – perhaps he plays it too well since he takes himself seriously. But eventually his own opinion of himself is
deflated. He finishes in the poorhouse: 'cette maison sert
souvent de retraite aux beaux esprits' (p. 553). He has decided
to give up writing poetry and to abandon the muses. He
states, apparently unaware of the comic contradiction, 'quand
tu es entré dans cette salle, je composais des vers pour leur
dire un éternel adieu' (p. 554). As Laufer points out, Fabrice,
at the end of the novel, has become the mouthpiece for
Lesage himself: 'j'ai pris le public en aversion. Il ne mérite
pas qu'il y ait des auteurs qui veuillent lui consacrer leurs
travaux' (p. 554). The view expressed is one of bitterness and
resentment. What Lesage appears to be saying is that contem-

porary popularity is worth little: it serves to bolster the pride
of authors. But the only real guide to quality is that which is
long-lasting, and this is something which contemporaries are
ill-equipped to predict. It is also, of course, the perfect
defence of an unsuccessful writer. The same idea is stated
more pointedly, as we shall see, in the portrait of Gabriel
Triaquero, normally considered to be Voltaire.

Fabrice makes a come-back, however. Don Bertrand
Gomez del Ribero needed a poet to write his 'billets galants'.
Fabrice got the job and is now prostituting his 'art' with
considerable success. Moreover, his play, written on an idea
inspired by his rich patron, was such a dreadful flop that don
Bertrand, staggered at the bad taste of the public, had decided
to reward the unfortunate author with a pension for life. As
Fabrice now realises only too well, quality and success do not
always go hand in hand. He is lucid enough at the end to
conclude: 'les sifflets m'ont mis tout d'un coup à mon aise
pour le reste de mes jours' (p. 562).

Scipion too remarks on the nature of fate which rewards
mediocrity and is harsh towards quality (p. 562). The point
has been made clearly enough and the personal nature of
Lesage's novel is apparent through the character of Fabrice.
His financial stability is short-lived, through no fault of
his own, and he finishes his life in mediocrity, happy
with his lot, living a life of independence and without am-
bitious pretentions. Fabrice's conclusions are not dissimilar
to those of Gil himself. Chance and fate determine one's
life, not merit and quality. In such a world ambition plays
little part.

(vi) *The Theatre*

The novel is full of allusions and references to the world
of the theatre, and there can be no doubt that there must be a
relationship between this emphasis and the meaning of the
text as a whole. It is apparent, throughout the novel, that
Lesage is saying that the theatre is not simply to be found on
the stage. Critics have disagreed about the significance of the
theatrical elements (see especially, *15,* p. 144).

Whatever meaning such episodes may have, one cannot escape the conclusion that the world of the theatre is, of all the worlds described by Gil, the one which appears to be most authentic and most personally motivated. It is, I think, the satire of the theatre and of actors generally which is the most effective. We see actors constantly criticising the authors who supply them with their conditions of livelihood. Book III, Chapter XI (pp. 171-74) is devoted almost entirely to an analysis of the relationship between actors and authors. At the end of the meal an author arrives: the company of actors treats him with scorn and obvious superiority. His reaction is one of fear and embarrassment. When he leaves, the conversation turns to more general comments about authors: 'Les auteurs sont-ils dignes de notre attention? [. . .] Traitons-les toujours en esclaves, et ne craignons point de lasser leur patience' (p. 174). Gil concludes the chapter with apparent objectivity: 'Ces histrions les mettaient au-dessous d'eux, et certes ils ne pouvaient les mépriser davantage' (p. 174).

It is apparent, throughout the novel, that Lesage bears a grudge against the 'official' theatre. The Théâtre du Prince (du Roi?) contains actors who deserve to be on the road but who have entered the troupe out of favour, as Melchior Zapata points out (p. 122). Don Pompeyo de Castro, an objective observer from Portugal, is asked to comment on the acting performance he has seen at the Théâtre du Prince. Fashion plays no part in his ambitions as he enumerates the actors and actresses he has seen, stressing particularly their inability to appear natural on stage. The audience, he maintains, is not always the best judge of quality ('Il applaudit même plus rarement au vrai mérite qu'au faux', p. 155), and he introduces the comic anecdote about the peasant and the pig (pp. 155-66).

In his presentation of the theatre Lesage is making the same general statement as the one he made about literature: There is no guarantee that merit will bring success. Actors and actresses have inflated views of their own importance; they are unable to see the true nature of the roles they are playing in society. As I shall suggest in my final chapter, it is

the theatrical metaphor which points to the essential meaning
of the novel.

(vii) *'Real' Figures*

As I have already remarked, the illusion of Spain is
constantly contradicted by allusions to French reality. The
comic satire of *littérateurs* and *comédiens* is both of a general
and a personal nature. The fictional characters introduced by
Lesage have clear 'real' counterparts (see especially the useful
notes in the Laufer edition, pp. 621-30, for information about
the identity of characters). It is essentially, but not entirely,
the world of literature, taken in its broadest sense, which
provides these characters. The most obvious one, and the one
which did most to harm Lesage's reputation, is Gabriel
Triaquero, otherwise known as Voltaire. Voltaire, offended
by his portrait in *Gil Blas,* accused Lesage of having taken the
novel entirely from *La vida del escudero don Marcos de
Obregón* and the accusation was not fully dismissed until
some one hundred years later, in the edition of the novel by the
comte de Neufchâteau. It is not surprising that Voltaire took
exception to his portrait. Gil goes to see the first performance
of a play by this 'poète à la mode' (p. 483). The theatre is
fully booked in advance, such is the reputation of Gabriel,
and the play is, of course, a resounding success. The author
goes 'modestement' from box to box to receive his praise
(p. 487). After the performance Gil returns to dine at don
Alphonse's palace. There is one dissenting voice from the
praise heaped on the new play: a 'gentilhomme de Madrid,
qui avait de l'esprit et du goût' (p. 484). Clearly his opinion
is going to be significant: he wishes to reserve his judgement.
Quality is *not* apparent simply from one performance of the
play, he claims. The play must be read if its full value is to be
appreciated. The implication is, very clearly, that Gabriel is
praised too readily out of pure fashion. Another *cavalier*
disagrees: 'Il suffit que nous sachions que c'est une produc-
tion de don Gabriel pour être persuadés qu'elle est sans
défaut' (p. 484). The gentilhomme de Madrid, prompted by
the ridiculous statement of the *cavalier,* starts to criticise the

play with severity: 'C'est un poème farci de traits plus brillants que solides. Les trois quarts des vers sont mauvais ou mal rimés, les caractères mal formés ou mal soutenus, et les pensées souvent très obscures' (pp. 484-85). Lesage is careful to assert that his critic is both intelligent and of good taste. His remarks are damning indeed, and Voltaire would have felt peeved with reason. The most successful tragedian of the period was being humbled by a writer of novels and comedies, and called, no doubt much to his distaste, 'ce nouveau nourrisson des Muses' (p. 485). Lesage's short chapter no doubt expresses his own jealousy of Voltaire's success, and at the same time he underlines the view that while fashion may define success, literary merit will lie with posterity. One might conclude that Lesage was at least partly justified: Voltaire's tragedies are rarely performed or read today.

Lesage uses *Gil Blas* to express a satirical view of his own dislikes and antagonisms. The characters we can now identify would have been immediately recognisable to a contemporary readership, but the novel can still be enjoyed even if the 'real' characters remain purely fictional. One of the most striking portraits in the novel is the one of Carlos Alonso de la Ventoleria (pp. 171-72), given by Laure, who is said to represent the actor-author Baron, a rival and enemy of Lesage. He is old, dyes his hair, and claims to be twenty years younger than he is. He is conceited and self-satisfied, vain and affected. The character is described in such detail that the reader has no trouble in imagining him in real life. Contemporary readers would have picked up the one obvious clue to his identity: he had left the stage and returned much later. The satire is comic in its exaggeration, yet colourful and effective. It is clearly double-edged.

Such is the case for the other characters in the novel who are said to represent real figures. They add variety and colour to the novel: they are precisely described in a way that obviously fictional characters are not. And the illusion benefits consequentially. Boindin, the critic, is introduced as 'un petit homme' (p. 215). In Scipion's story Scipion works for don Ignacio de Ipigna (Bouhours) an author who has a unique method of composition: he writes down on cards the apohthegms he reads in classical authors, and when they are full he threads them on to metal wire, makes a garland of them, and each garland constitutes a volume: 'Que nous faisions de mauvais livres! Il ne se passait guère de mois que nous ne fissions pour le moins deux volumes, et aussitôt la presse en gémissait' (p. 533).

Gil Blas is not, I think, a *livre à clef,* but Lesage introduces 'real' figures when they can appear naturally in the text and enhance the comedy. I suspect that a number of characters have not been identified who may well, originally, have been contemporary figures of satire. The transposition of reality into fiction allows the author to increase the range of his comic vision.

COMIC SCENES

It has been said that Lesage the novelist is never far removed from Lesage the playwright.[2] Lesage's great skill in *Gil Blas* is in imagining a number of highly dramatic scenes whose main function is to make us laugh, normally at the expense of Gil himself. This is the crucial element of comedy and one which defines humour in the novel. We laugh at Gil and find him sympathetic because he is now, retrospectively, able to laugh at himself. We laugh at others and reject them because they take themselves too seriously.

A number of scenes remain vividly in the mind: Gil responding to the archevêque de Grenade's appeal to be warned when his age adversely affects his capacity to write (he does so and is promptly sacked (pp. 321-31), but the lesson in human nature is worth the loss of occupation); Gil's completely wrong assessment of Camille and her advances towards him, which we pick up very early on (pp. 67-71); the meeting with don Annibal de Chinchilla and the comic description of him ('Outre qu'il lui manquait un bras et une jambe, il avait la place d'un œil couverte d'une large emplâtre de taffetas vert, et son visage en plusieurs endroits parais-

[2] F. C. Green, *Minuet* (London, Dent, 1935), p. 348.

sait balafré. A cela près, il était fait comme un autre',
pp. 356-57); Gil's wrong assessment of his mistress Aurore,
whom he assumes to be in love with him (pp. 179-85). He
spends all his money on creams, perfume and clothes, arrives
for the rendezvous covered in lotion two hours too early and
imagines, with obvious anticipation, the delightful scenes
which are to follow. He tries to recall the plays he has seen
which might include a scene he could make use of in the
present circumstances, but when he arrives his mistress
laughs at his antics – she wants him simply as a go-between.
The hero is suitably deflated and proved to be quite wrong
in his appreciation ot the true situation. He invites laughter
and gets his due.

It is when Gil shows himself to be less than heroic that we
are most amused at him: he leaves Valladolid in a hurry to
avoid a possible fight; in the showdown with his rival for the
hand of Lorenza Séphora, whom he cares little about, we see
Gil Blas mechanically responding to expectation: he is supposed to be angry and seeking revenge. He confronts his rival:
'Je me mis à considérer mon homme, qui me sembla fort
vigoureux; et je trouvai son épée d'une longueur excessive'
(p. 317), and is only too pleased to find a good reason not to
fight. Gil is not the dashing hero of the adventure story: he is
the ordinary, normal human being who is seeking to improve
his lot. He remains in our affection because of his fallibility
and this capacity to laugh at himself.

Lesage does not miss a trick in this comic novel: the irony
of the narrator looking back and describing himself with
detachment but in the knowledge of ultimate contentment
lends itself to comedy; the use of certain forms of language
and the witty phrase are constant comic factors: Gil Blas goes
to sleep 'en bâtissant des châteaux en Espagne' (p. 352); the
proverb 'Tu es du bois dont on fait les flûtes' becomes, in the
language of Manuel Ordoñez, 'Tu es du bois dont on fait les
économes' (p. 364). But it is Gil's ability to laugh at himself
which provides the essence of comedy in the novel. At the
end, his future assured, he spends three hours getting ready
for his wedding: 'Pour un adolescent que se prépare à voir sa
maîtresse, ce n'est qu'un plaisir; mais pour un homme qui

commence à vieillir, c'est une occupation' (p. 608). The final
phrase in the novel as he refers to his two children 'dont je
crois pieusement être le père' (p. 609) alerts us to the fact that
even in this sentimental ending Gil cannot avoid a slanted
remark about himself. It is clearly time to analyse in more
detail the character of Gil. He is the dynamic force of the
novel. The comedy revolves around his account of the world
and his confrontation with it. Gil, unlike the figures of satire,
is mobile and free. He moves through different social echelons providing us with a seemingly detached view of the
reality he observes. The comic element is stronger when the
distance between Gil and his current reality is greatest; as he
starts to mature and to become part of the social world he had
previously mocked, so the comedy of the novel diminishes.
Gil, to the end, is unaware of the assessment we are likely to
make of him. He conveniently forgets his past when he
observes his present reality, but we, as readers, view Gil with
a detachment which may well be more critical than he,
through his account, would have desired.

6

The Character of Gil

IN an analysis of the satirical intentions of *Gil Blas* it is easy
to concentrate on the view of reality expressed by Gil the
narrator and to forget that he too, in his remarks about
himself, is lending himself as an object of satire. As he
ascends the echelons of society he remains, simultaneously,
both his new self and his past self in the mind of the reader.
Dédéyan emphasises Gil's *naïveté,* his 'candeur', his 'fran-
chise' (*4,* II, ch. XV) but it is his *inability* to see himself as *we*
see him which represents his greatest interest for the reader.
Lesage's 'realism' is related to his creation of a character who
is like us. We are willing and able to criticise others but are
rarely, if ever, aware of the view that others will have of us.
The dialogue between Gil and the reader is paralleled by a
dialogue between Lesage and the reader, using Gil as the
channel of communication. Indeed, the irony of the novel
depends on our assessment of Gil Blas. It may not correspond
to the assessment he makes of himself.

Gil is unlikely to present the reader with a constant
critique of his own character. His account is, as I have
already said, a kind of confession, but the sins which are
openly confessed appear trivial against the sins which are
mentioned but to which our attention is not drawn specifically.

Gil undergoes an educative process in the course of
events. He soon realises that crime does not pay and prefers
to remain a servant rather than join Rolando, (p. 136), even
though Rolando says he despises the 'bassesse de tes inclina-
tions' (ibid.). When he is dismissed from the services of the
archevêque de Grenade, Melchior de la Ronda spells out the
important lesson he should learn from the incident: 'Les

hommes du commun doivent toujours respecter les hommes
de qualité, quelque sujet qu'ils aient de s'en plaindre' (p. 331).
Gil notes the incident and relates it as if it has modified
his perception of reality: he simply fails to perceive that his
final being is not greatly different from his initial being. He
thinks the Gil Blas who looks back on Gil Blas is an
improved, educated, noble figure. We know differently: he
describes his changing status but is never able to detach
himself sufficiently from his past to break away from it. The
political power he has exerted is no proof of status: nobility
cannot be acquired.

Certainly, in his account of the past, he is able to offer a
retrospective view of himself which appears to indicate a
difference between the two Gils, hero and narrator. The
trivial incidents in which he is duped or outwitted – by the
parasite at Peñaflor (p. 28), by Camille (pp. 67-71), and by
don Bernard (p. 137) – appear to be showing that Gil is
gradually learning to perceive the nature of the world and to
be developing in his capacity to respond to it. But he never
dominates reality: he remains, from beginning to end, an
underling, and one senses that the valet Scipion is actually
more perceptive than he is himself. The real *pícaro* is better
equipped to deal with reality than the false noble.

In his account of his character, Gil seems to be saying that
he has learnt all there is to learn about life; there are
occasions when he admits his past errors with a certain relish:
for example, his wrong assessment of the admiration Béatrix
shows towards him: 'Je m'imaginai donc que j'avais fait la
conquête d'une vieille suivante, et je me trompai encore dans
cette occasion' (p. 224). He admits the mistake he made in
telling his master too readily that Eufrasie had another lover:
'Que j'étais fat, quand j'y pense, de raisonner de la sorte!'
(p. 226). The retrospective nature of the account is emphasised
by these judgements of past actions and by his apparent
willingness to laugh at his past physical appearance: he
describes his 'sotte figure' (p. 362) at Court and appears to be
suggesting, now, that the situation is quite different. But his
complacency at the end of the novel contradicts the message
which has been constant throughout the account, that man

does not control his own destiny: 'Je suis né pour être le jouet de la fortune' (p. 320). The three years of 'delightful' life appear to be no guarantee of future security, if past events are to be seen as indicative.

It is Fabrice, friend and confidant, who is the best guide to our assessment of Gil Blas. He serves as a constant comparison, representing both what Gil is and pointing out what he might have been. Gil does not see that Fabrice is just as reliable a model of humanity as he himself is. Indeed, it is Fabrice who stresses the duality of Gil Blas. At the moment of living the experience of being secretary to the duc de Lerme, Gil assumes, quite wrongly, that he is now part of the nobility he is serving (p. 424). It is Fabrice who assesses the new reality which Gil retrospectively now reports to us: 'Gil Blas n'est plus ce même Gil Blas que j'ai connu'. Gil is unable to respond to this attack and says simply: 'Tu plaisantes sans doute' (p. 425). Fabrice then points out to Gil a message which he is never able to understand and yet which we, as readers, are bound to pick up and use in our analysis of character: 'Ce n'est point à tes yeux [. . .] qu'on doit s'en rapporter. Ils sont fascinés. Crois-moi, ta métamorphose n'est que trop véritable' (pp. 425-26). The message *appears* to have been learnt, since the event is recounted with obvious embarrassment and distaste. But the criticism remains in the reader's mind as a constant factor of judgement. Gil Blas is never a good witness of Gil Blas: he failed to see himself clearly at the moment of the event, and his perception of the past is dulled by his awareness of the present. The same might be said of any first-person narrative. The reader will normally find Gil Blas to be a sympathetic, human figure who has vices and virtues as we all do, but such a conclusion will depend on reading the text as an authentic account given by the hero. What I am suggesting is that Lesage is supplying the reader with a double reading: we read Gil's account of himself; and we read Lesage's account of Gil. The two accounts simply fail to coincide. It is the first reading which will strike us immediately. Gil's account of himself is essentially an account of certain episodes in his life, the educative process he went through, and the conclusions he has now

made about life, based on his adventures. Gil appears as a
sensitive man, by nature. He cries at the tragic tale of doña
Mencia (p. 56), claims to be *basically* honest (his distaste for
the life of the highwaymen), and essentially virtuous (his
sexual morality towards Antonia, pointed out by Scipion):
'Tous les seigneurs de village à votre place n'en useraient pas
si honnêtement; ils n'auraient sur Antonia des vues légitimes
qu'après en avoir eu d'autres inutilement' (p. 493). Now, in
retrospect, he expresses regret at having killed off the patients
while working for Sangrado (p. 466). He readily admits those
faults which we are likely to notice for ourselves. He is
remorseful for the way he abandoned his poor parents and is
harshly treated by the villagers at his father's funeral who are
'choqués de mon ostentation' (p. 474). Certainly, Gil appears
to have undergone a moral transformation in the course of
the novel. He has now a moral awareness which, previously,
he had not. But there remains an insoluble problem. Gil Blas
assumes now that he is a superior being: he feels that the new
Gil Blas, experienced and noble, transcends the old one. I
suspect that Lesage is saying just the opposite. At the end of
the novel, when Gil is given his 'lettres de noblesse' (p. 591),
he claims that such an honour does not make him proud. But
the expression he uses suggests exactly the contrary: 'J'ose
dire à ma louange qu'elles ne m'inspirèrent aucun orgueil.
Ayant toujours devant les yeux la bassesse de mon origine,
cet honneur m'humiliait au lieu de me donner de la vanité'
(p. 592). Gil is proud to say he is not proud! One senses a
certain superiority in the complacency of the final chapter. It
may be that as we come to know Gil better so our relationship with him becomes more distant. We are more likely to
find attractive a young man struggling for survival in the
jungle of society than an older man who stands aloof and is
proud of his financial security.

The ageing process which Gil's account emphasises re-
flects our distanciation from him. In his youth and in his
struggle to become something, we can admire Gil for his
ingenuity and pity him for his misfortunes. When he accedes
to power and simply copies other powerful figures in his
corruption and ambition he loses our sympathy, but he does

not realise the fact. He calls us 'ami lecteur' in the final paragraph but the truth is that we have become more critical of him as the distance between his past self and his present self diminishes. He claims constantly that the experience of power which he describes while working for d'Olivarès is different from the one with the duc de Lerme. He maintains that he seeks, under d'Olivarès, a good position but one which will not allow him 'un honteux trafic des bienfaits du prince' (p. 542). He claims, in his account of the favour offered to don André de Tordesillas, 'que je n'étais plus ce même Gil Blas qui sous le ministère précédent vendait les grâces de la Cour' (p. 566). As the novel draws to a conclusion so the two characters of Gil, then and now, merge into one. And so the language of perception becomes more complex and more awkward. The difficulty is apparent in Gil's description of himself in the final chapter: 'Quoique je ne parusse pas avoir mon âge et que je pusse me donner dix bonnes années moins que je n'en avais, je ne laissais pas de me croire bien fondé à douter que je plusse à une jeune beauté' (p. 607). As we observe Gil Blas settling down into respectability we are led to the conclusion that he was more interesting when vice was a constant temptation. His announcement to Fabrice, 'Les disgrâces [. . .] ont purifié ma vertu; et j'ai appris à l'école de l'adversité à jouir des richesses sans m'en laisser posséder' (pp. 553-54) guarantees a moral conclusion to the novel. But a moral conclusion may be what the reader desires least in a novel like *Gil Blas*.

Gil Blas and Meaning

GIL BLAS is a compendium of ideas on human nature, on morality and on the ways of the world. In an attempt to concentrate exclusively on one major theme there is an obvious risk of disservice. Through a multitude of characters, Lesage is putting forward diverse ideas. If one were to concentrate solely on Gil himself one might be tempted to conclude that the novel is an extended moral tale where, eventually, virtue leads to happiness. But I have already raised doubts about such an interpretation and suspect that this is not Lesage's meaning or intention.

One very obvious aim of the novel is to satirise those elements of society which most deserve critical analysis; institutions and individuals are included in this category. The very fabric of society and the prejudices on which it is based come under attack. As I have already indicated, Gil is not excluded from this satire: in his attempt to be something he patently can never be, he leaves himself vulnerable. Marivaux's peasant in *Le Paysan parvenu* shows the same desire to climb the ranks of society. But at the end he remains, at least in definition, a modified peasant, not a new character. Gil Blas wrongly assumes that each past action and state can be excluded in a view of the present: the reappearance of his parents reminds us, if not him, of his lowly origins. Gil will never be the real noble he is proud to claim to be.

Indeed, worse than that, as Gil moves upwards, still in service, he is lucid enough to perceive the empty world of corruption which is common in all classes, but he still hopes to attain the rank he is criticising and eventually to transcend it. His snobbery is particularly apparent after the 'petits-maîtres' episode. He claims he is charmed by their wit and despairs at ever being able to resemble them (p. 144), failing to see their parasitical nature and their empty existence. Indeed, he has taken on airs of his own: 'Je ne voulais plus servir que des personnes hors du commun' (p. 165), and 'J'ai juré [. . .] de ne plus servir de bourgeois' (p. 166). In the end he agrees to serve a *comédienne,* gullibly accepting the preposterous view that an actor can be seen to equal the nobility and even, on occasions, to represent a monarch.

As Gil serves richer and more powerful masters so his scorn for the bourgeoisie increases. His first reaction at Scipion's suggestion that he should marry the daughter of a rich goldsmith is, quite simply, 'Peux-tu me proposer une bourgeoise?' (p. 427). Gil has forgotten that merit and value in society are not related to condition. It is a point made by Scipion in the consideration of his daughter's marriage: 'J'estime moins la noblesse [. . .] que les qualités du cœur et de l'esprit, et ce don Juan nous conviendra si c'est un honnête homme' (p. 605). This surely, then, is one meaning of the novel. It is a message which Gil loses sight of as he moves upward. Indeed, it is evident to us, even by observing Gil Blas himself, that merit is of little significance in the establishment of the social hierarchy. His position of power with d'Olivarès is obtained by his friend Navarro via his uncle, don Baltazar Zuñiga (p. 548).

If *Gil Blas* can be seen as a moral novel it must be considered a particularly depressing one. Success and happiness are the lot of those with friends in high places rather than the natural rewards of the world. A good example of such unfairness is the hero, don Annibal (pp. 356-61). The novel abounds with moral statements which seem, at first sight at least, to be significant. The captain of the brigands, Rolando, claims: 'tous les hommes aiment à s'approprier le bien d'autrui. C'est un sentiment général. La manière seule en est différente' (p. 39), but the fact that he is a robber makes us view his apparently objective statements with a certain scepticism.

Gil has learnt, in the course of his experiences, that self-interest is the motivating factor in human activity. In his attempt to rehabilitate Louis Garcias, Gil realises that

success will depend on his appeal to the archbishop's vanity
(p. 328). He sees, in his own conduct, that his willingness to
criticise the disgraced duc de Lerme is indicative of the
self-interest which dominates: 'Voilà l'homme' (p. 549) he
concludes with resignation. The moral statements which we
find scattered throughout the novel have in common their
banality. Money corrupts (p. 461), pride will lead to a fall
(p. 476) and virtue alone brings happiness: 'Rien n'est tel que
de vivre en repos' (p. 351). But these statements do not, in my
opinion, constitute the real meaning of the work.

There is a theme which we find throughout and which, I
think, points to the only consistent message of the novel, both
in the main body of the text and in the interpolated stories.
Lesage, through the character of Gil, is showing us that
maturity and insight are defined by the ability to distinguish
between the appearance of reality and reality itself. It is this
theme which, I suggest, explains the very high incidence of
theatrical language and the unusually large number of actors
and actresses playing important parts in Gil's reality. Furthermore, I would suggest, more tentatively, that Gil's 'ad-
vancement' in the novel is reflected by his gradual loss of
awareness of his own role: in other words, at the end of the
novel he thinks he is something he is not.

Early in the account, when Gil describes his capture by
the brigands and gives details of his escape, he realises that
his success depends on his ability to convince the villains of
the reality of his illness: 'Je feignis d'avoir la colique. Je
poussai d'abord des plaintes et des gémissements [. . .] En un
mot je jouai si bien mon rôle, que les voleurs, tout fins qu'ils
étaient, s'y laissèrent tromper' (p. 48). When Fabrice tells Gil
of his successful post with Manuel Ordoñez, he too emphasises the need to appear to be something he is not. The
language he uses is that of the theatre: 'Je le copiai, et, jouant
devant lui le même rôle qu'il fait devant les autres, je trompai
le trompeur et je suis devenu peu à peu son *factoton*' (p. 74).

It is the language of the theatre which dominates the
novel. As Gil adopts various roles to perfection, so his status
changes and his wealth increases. When he first seduces
Laure he is dressed as an 'homme de Cour' (p. 149), but fails

to realise that Laure too is disguised. In the episode where Aurore is disguised as a man to spy more easily on the one she loves, don Luis, and in order to bring him round to admiring her, Gil constantly refers to the events as a 'comédie': 'Nous choisîmes nos acteurs dans le domestique, puis nous distribuâmes les rôles. Ce qui se passa sans clameurs et sans querelles, parce que nous n'étions pas des comédiens de profession' (p. 187).

The language of theatre is used consistently to describe reality. Nowhere is this more true than in the Aurore episode (pp. 208-20). This incident, in which Gil plays a major part, is an important formative experience. Gil realises that his social progress is directly related to his capacity to convince. If he can produce the perfect acting performance he will gain his due rewards. However, as he progresses, so the disparity between what he is and what he appears to be diminishes. In his most important role he becomes totally corrupt: he *is* the person he was trying to be. The moment of crisis precedes his allegorical tale to the duc de Lerme. 'J'étais toute la journée sur mon théâtre, c'est-à-dire, chez le duc; j'y jouais un rôle de seigneur. Mais quand j'étais retiré dans mon taudis, le seigneur s'évanouissait, et il ne restait que le pauvre Gil Blas, sans argent' (p. 395). The moment that his income matches the part he is playing, the distinction between reality and pretence disappears. Gil Blas *is* the secretary to the duc de Lerme and he forgets the real Gil Blas. Indeed, as the emphasis of the novel changes and we observe Gil Blas in positions of power, so the language of the theatre diminishes. Gil is no longer conscious of the role he is playing. He appears to believe that imitation has no further use. This change of emphasis coincides with our loss of affection for the hero. The novel includes, as I have said, an uncanny number of theatrical episodes. Many of these relate to specific satire, but it becomes apparent to the reader that the best actors are not always on stage. Two characters stand out as actors of great quality on every occasion that we see them: Don Raphaël and Ambroise Lamela. Furthermore, such is their ability to convince that even when Gil knows them perfectly he can be taken in by them. Their roles in the novel are obviously of great significance, and their reappearances serve as a gauge of Gil's awareness. He fails the test miserably and appears not to appreciate his own lack of insight.

When Ambroise is first introduced to Gil by Majuelo, Gil fails to pick up the true sense of Majuelo's advice. Gil intends to go to Madrid to make his fortune. Majuelo says: 'On juge là comme ailleurs sur les apparences et vous n'y serez considéré qu'à proportion de la figure qu'on vous verra faire' (p. 66). What Majuelo says proves to be true, but Gil fails to see that he is falling head first into a trap. Ambroise is introduced: 'C'était un garçon de trente ans qui avait l'air simple et dévot' (p. 66); 'il me répondit d'un air pieux' (p. 67). We suspect that Ambroise is not all he appears to be. Gil, at the time, is completely taken in by Ambroise's admission that he is not interested in money and would take whatever Gil cared to give him (p. 66).

Retrospectively, Gil can afford to laugh at himself now. But on every occasion when he meets Ambroise he makes the same mistake. Clearly, Ambroise and don Raphaël possess a quality which Gil singularly fails to possess. They are masters of deception, totally conscious of the roles they are playing and manipulating their audience with ease. Towards the end of the novel we assume that Gil is no longer the foolish, imperceptive, credulous youth he once was, unable to distinguish good from bad, truth from dishonesty. He gives the appearance of gaining control, of increasing in stature. But Lesage is showing us very clearly that Gil never dominates reality in the way he thinks he does. He quite simply forgets not only that *he* is playing a role but that others are too. Lesage is not only saying that the world is a stage; he is also showing us that, to the end, Gil Blas is capable of the most crass misjudgement. Don Raphaël's significance in the novel should not be underestimated: at a crucial moment in its development our attention is taken away from Gil and directed towards him.

Don Raphaël has fooled Gil Blas a second time when he tells him his life-story. He fools the readers too, on a first reading, since few will pick up the clue 'Venez, mes enfants, répondit l'anachorète après m'avoir regardé avec attention'

(p. 233). His identity is revealed, somewhat lamely, later on: 'Mais représentez-vous ma surprise, lorsque je reconnus dans le vieil anachorète le seigneur don Raphaël' (p. 245). As don Raphaël tells his story we realise that he is a master of disguise, and most adept at escaping from the most unlikely difficulties. He has a wit and an awareness that Gil cannot match, which may well explain Gil's comment that his story is a bit long (p. 295).

He reappears in the 1735 *livraison,* and this time Gil recognises him by his physical appearance. Don Raphaël and Ambroise have become Carthusian monks, much to the satisfaction of Gil. As Ambroise explains their conversion the reader is looking for clues to the truth, just as Gil is. Does Ambroise overstate his case? 'Ce qu'il y a de plus surprenant, c'est que, malgré le soin dont il est chargé de recueillir nos revenus, il ne paraît occupé que de l'éternité' (p. 487). He certainly convinces Gil, but we remain suspicious, just as don Alphonse does. Don Alphonse's reaction to Gil's account is indicative: 'Je n'aime pas que la caisse du couvent soit entre les mains de ce père Hilaire, dont je ne puis m'empêcher de me défier' (p. 489). His distrust proves to be well justified. Some days later the two villains escape with the money. Were they ever sincere in their conversion or did the temptation prove too great? We just do not know. Much later we see them going to their execution by the Inquisition and virtue is satisfied: 'Le Ciel, las des désordres de la vie de ces deux scélérats, les a donc livrés à la justice de l'Inquisition!' (p. 576). Gil recognises that he too might have finished that way. But he fails to realise that he never attained the perfection of performance of the two experts, nor, to his discredit, did he ever manage to distinguish the reality behind the appearance. We are reminded, in our search for a meaning which can explain and unify the disparate elements of the novel, of the anecdote of the theatre told by don Pompeyo and overheard by Gil. A peasant claims that an actor's imitation of a pig is poor and boasts that he can do better. The next day the two compete to see who can offer the best imitation: the well-known actor is applauded and the peasant mocked, at which point the peasant produces a *real* pig. The audience had preferred the imitation to the real thing, because their judgement was based on prejudice. The audience must be scorned for its lack of perception.

Is it possible to use this fable as a guide to an interpretation of the novel? Real value, real nobility come when appearance and reality coincide perfectly. It is a sign of quality to realise the distinction between appearing and being, and this quality is never attained by Gil. Certainly he has progressed considerably since the youthful days of *naïveté* and innocence. But he is not lucid enough at the end to understand that his final position in life is not guaranteed eternally, nor can it be said to reflect the merit he thinks he has. By such a minute account of his past we are offered an intimate account of his weaknesses. Chance, not merit, has brought success – Lesage is telling us this through his character – but poor Gil does not appear to be aware of it. If the novel had finished in 1715 our attitude to Gil would have been sympathetic; by 1735 he had changed so much that, without realising it, he was distancing himself from the reader and losing his affection.

Our final view of Gil sees him desperately making himself up to appear younger than he really is. He fails to produce a satisfactory result. At the end of the novel Gil Blas character is the same as Gil Blas narrator: he cannot rediscover youth nor can he appear to be something he is not. As the novel finishes so the reader appreciates that Gil Blas has allowed his past to catch up with him: there is no comedy in the final chapter, simply a sad reminder that Gil is no more the alert, lively, amusing figure he once was. There is no longer any narrative perspective and, without distance, the comedy disappears and sentimentality takes its place.

Conclusion

T H E R E is not one conclusion to this study, but several are
possible: it seems clear to me that Lesage was a much more
'aware' novelist than he is normally considered to be. He
understands the limits and capacity of first-person fiction and
uses the form with particular, ironical intent. The result is a
self-conscious novel of sorts, and one which has a clearly
satirical intention.

I do not consider *Gil Blas* to be a didactic novel, in spite
of the introductory 'Gil Blas au lecteur', since the moral is
not intended for us but is used as a means of examining the
central figure. There are a number of possible meanings, but
one view predominates: people are generally corrupt and
hypocritical, but some are more so than others.

Lesage is sometimes considered to be an early realist
because he includes many 'low' characters and produces a
convincing illusion of reality. I find this view difficult to
accept, not least because the illusion of Spain is *constantly*
broken. Lesage is aware of many of the technical problems
which beset the first-person narrator, the most obvious of
which is knowledge. He makes some attempts to cope with
the problem and so could be called more 'realistic' than some
other contemporary writers.

The novel was an immense success and was republished
throughout the eighteenth and nineteenth centuries. It was an
important text in the development of French fiction. It is not
really a picaresque novel – any more than *Tom Jones* is – but
it does have the quality of movement and the episodic
structure of the picaresque. No doubt Marivaux had *Gil Blas*
in mind when he wrote his *Paysan parvenu*. But there is
an important distinction: Gil Blas does not appear to be a

licentious hero; he does eventually fall in love, but it appears to be almost an afterthought by Lesage, an attempt to include an ingredient at a late stage. Voltaire knew *Gil Blas,* disliked Lesage and tried to harm the reputation of both. It is in his *Candide* that we find the most obvious reminder of *Gil Blas.* The two Inquisition scenes need to be compared – *Gil Blas,* pp. 575-76/*Candide,* Ch. 6 – and one cannot read the decision of d'Olivarès to leave the Court and retire to the country without thinking of the conclusion to *Candide:* 'Monseigneur, pour varier ses occupations, s'amusait aussi quelquefois à cultiver son jardin' (p. 599).

Select Bibliography

L A U F E R ' S edition in the Garnier-Flammarion collection, no. 286, has been chosen as a reliable text with useful notes and helpful meanings of names for non-Hispanists. The edition by Etiemble, in *Romanciers du 18e siècle*, Vol. I (Paris, Gallimard, Bibliothèque de la Pléiade, 1960), pp. 491-1197, reproduced in the Folio edition, nos. 498-499 (Paris, Gallimard, 1973), which is based on the text published by the Veuve Ribou from 1732 to 1737, is, in a sense, less authentic than the Laufer edition based on a corrected version of the 1715 text (Tomes I and II), the 1724 text and a corrected version of the 1735 text.

CRITICAL WORKS

1. K. Whitman Carson, 'Aspects of Contemporary Society in *Gil Blas*', *Studies on Voltaire and the Eighteenth Century*, CX, 1973. Attempts to provide a survey of the picture of society in the novel. Not very critical and somewhat anecdotal.
2. C. Cavillac, *L'Espagne dans la trilogie 'picaresque' de Lesage. Emprunts littéraires, empreinte culturelle* (Bordeaux, Presses Universitaires, 1984), 2 vols. A major study of Lesage which, in a remarkable synthesis, shows both the author's debts to Spain and Spanish literature, and his own particular originality.
3. L. Claretie, *Essai sur Lesage romancier* (Paris, Armand Colin, 1890). Both a biography of Lesage and a critical assessment of his novels. Difficult to fault, but mainly uninspired.
4. C. Dédéyan, *Lesage and 'Gil Blas'* (Paris, SEDES, 1965), 2 vols. A long, complete, laborious account of the novel which tends to recount the story with little critical insight.
5. M.-H. Huet, *Le Héros et son double. Essai sur le roman d'ascension sociale au XVIIIe siècle* (Paris, Corti, 1975). See especially pp. 11-30 for a study of *Gil Blas*. Lively, if not totally accurate account of Gil's social progress.
6. H. Klüppelholz, *La Technique des emprunts dans 'Gil Blas' de Lesage* (Frankfurt, Lang, Europäische Hochschulschriften, 1981). Sensible, critical account of the novel, now surpassed by *2* above.
7. R. Laufer, *Lesage, ou le métier de romancier* (Gallimard, Bibliothèque des Idées, 1971). See especially Chapter VII, pp. 283-384 for a study of

Gil Blas. Authoritative, sympathetic account concentrating on an analysis of the structure of the novel.

8. A. Le Breton, *Le Roman au dix-huitième siècle* (Paris, Société française d'imprimerie et de librairie, n.d.). Emphasises Lesage's satirical intentions, critical of the author's ability to convince.

9. E. Lintilhac, *Lesage* (Paris, Hachette, 1893). Useful critical biography.

10. J. Longhurst, 'Lesage and the Spanish tradition', in *Studies in Eighteenth-Century French Literature, presented to Robert Niklaus,* ed. J. H. Fox, M. H. Waddicor and D. A. Watts (University of Exeter, 1975), pp. 123-37. Wide-ranging article which raises more problems than it solves. Tries to prove that *Gil Blas* is a picaresque novel.

11. G. May, *Le Dilemme du roman au XVIIIe siècle* (Paris, PUF, 1963). Excellent survey of the period of composition which analyses critical views of the novel and novelists' responses.

12. J. Molino, 'Les six premiers livres de l'histoire de Gil Blas de Santillane', *Annales de la Faculté des Lettres d'Aix,* XLIV, 1968, pp. 81-101. Useful analysis of the structure of books I-VI of the novel.

13. ———, 'Du roman picaresque au roman philosophique. Les livres VII, VIII et IX de *Gil Blas*', in *Mélanges à la mémoire d'A. Joucla-Ruan* (Editions de l'Université de Provence, 1978), pp. 945-60. Emphasises the changing status of the novel as it continued in 1724.

14. V. G. Mylne, *The Eighteenth-Century French Novel. Techniques of Illusion* (Manchester University Press, 1965; revised edition, Cambridge University Press, 1981). See especially Chapter IV, pp. 49-72, 'Lesage and conventions' for a useful discussion of the novel in the context of the picaresque, satire and fictional memoirs.

15. ———, 'Structure and symbolism in *Gil Blas*', *French Studies,* XV, 1961, pp. 134-45. Challenges Wagner's interpretations of the novel and rejects the view that the novel presents the world as a stage.

16. A. Parker, *Literature and the delinquent. The picaresque novel in Spain and Europe, 1599-1753* (Edinburgh University Press, 1967). A useful background text which situates *Gil Blas* in the context of the picaresque novel.

17. J. Proust, 'Lesage ou le regard intérieur. Recherches sur la place et la fonction de la 'description' dans *Gil Blas*', *Beiträge zur französischen Aufklärung und zur Spanischen Literatur. Festgabe für Werner Krauss zum 70. Geburtstag,* ed. W. Bahner (Berlin, Akademie-Verlag, 1971), pp. 289-314. Most interesting article, pre-dating Robichez. Asks whether it is possible to distinguish between narrative and description – or rather 'pure' narrative and 'pure' description.

18. J. Robichez, 'Le refus de la description dans *Gil Blas*', *Travaux de Linguistique et de Littérature,* XIII, 1975, pp. 483-89. Attempts to explain the lack of physical description in the novel.

19. E. Showalter, Jr, *The Evolution of the French Novel, 1641-1782* (Princeton University Press, 1972). A highly critical assessment of *Gil Blas* in the context of other novels. The novel is weak because of the ambiguities of its point of view.

20. N. Wagner, 'Quelques cadres d'étude pour *Gil Blas*', *L'Information littéraire,* VIII, 1956, pp. 29-38. Useful guide to the common themes of the novel; too much emphasis on the idea that the novel is proposing the view that the world is a vast theatre of human comedy.

CRITICAL GUIDES TO FRENCH TEXTS

edited by
Roger Little, Wolfgang van Emden, David Williams

1. **David Bellos**. Balzac: La Cousine Bette
2. **Rosemarie Jones**. Camus: L'Etranger *and* La Chute
3. **W.D. Redfern**. Queneau: Zazie dans le métro
4. **R.C. Knight**. Corneille: Horace
5. **Christopher Todd**. Voltaire: Dictionnaire philosophique
6. **J.P. Little**. Beckett: En attendant Godot *and* Fin de partie
7. **Donald Adamson**. Balzac: Illusions perdues
8. **David Coward**. Duras: Moderato cantabile
9. **Michael Tilby**. Gide: Les Faux-Monnayeurs
10. **Vivienne Mylne**. Diderot: La Religieuse
11. **Elizabeth Fallaize**. Malraux: La Voie royale
12. **H.T. Barnwell**. Molière: Le Malade imaginaire
13. **Graham E. Rodmell**. Marivaux: Le Jeu de l'amour et du hasard *and* Les Fausses Confidences
14. **Keith Wren**. Hugo: Hernani *and* Ruy Blas
15. **Peter S. Noble**. Beroul's Tristan *and the* Folie de Berne
16. **Paula Clifford**. Marie de France: Lais
17. **David Coward**. Marivaux: La Vie de Marianne *and* Le Paysan parvenu
18. **J.H. Broome**. Molière: L'Ecole des femmes *and* Le Misanthrope
19. **B.G. Garnham**. Robbe-Grillet: Les Gommes *and* Le Voyeur
20. **J.P. Short**. Racine: Phèdre
21. **Robert Niklaus**. Beaumarchais: Le Mariage de Figaro
22. **Anthony Cheal Pugh**. Simon: Histoire
23. **Lucie Polak**. Chrétien de Troyes: Cligés
24. **John Cruickshank**. Pascal: Pensées
25. **Ceri Crossley**. Musset: Lorenzaccio
26. **J.W. Scott**. Madame de Lafayette: La Princesse de Clèves
27. **John Holyoake**. Montaigne: Essais
28. **Peter Jimack**. Rousseau: Emile
29. **Roger Little**. Rimbaud: Illuminations
30. **Barbara Wright and David Scott**. Baudelaire: La Fanfarlo *and* Le Spleen de Paris

31. **Haydn Mason.** Cyrano de Bergerac: L'Autre Monde
32. **Glyn S. Burgess.** Chrétien de Troyes: Erec et Enide
33. **S. Beynon John.** Anouilh: L'Alouette *and* Pauvre Bitos
34. **Robin Buss.** Vigny: Chatterton
35. **David Williams.** Rousseau: Les Rêveries du promeneur solitaire
36. **Ronnie Butler.** Zola: La Terre
37. **John Fox.** Villon: Poems
38. **C.E.J. Dolamore.** Ionesco: Rhinocéros
39. **Robert Lethbridge.** Maupassant: Pierre et Jean
40. **David Curtis.** Descartes: Discours de la Méthode
41. **Peter Cogman.** Hugo: Les Contemplations
42. **Rosemary Lloyd.** Mallarmé: Poésies
43. **M. Adereth.** Aragon: The Resistance Poems
44. **Keith Wren.** Vigny: Les Destinées
45. **Kathleen M. Hall and Margaret B. Wells.** Du Bellay: Poems
46. **Geoffrey Bremner.** Diderot: Jacques le fataliste
47. **Peter Dunwoodie.** Camus: L'Envers et l'Endroit *and* L'Exil et le Royaume
48. **Michael Sheringham.** Beckett: Molloy
49. **J.F. Falvey.** Diderot: Le Neveu de Rameau
50. **Dennis Fletcher.** Voltaire: Lettres philosophiques.
51. **Philip Robinson.** Bernardin de Saint-Pierre: Paul et Virginie
52. **Richard Griffiths.** Garnier: Les Juifves
53. **Paula Clifford.** La Chastelaine de Vergi *and* Jean Renart: Le Lai de l'ombre
54. **Robin Buss.** Cocteau: Les Enfants terribles
55. **Tony Hunt.** Chrétien de Troyes: Yvain
56. **Robert Gibson.** Alain-Fournier: Le Grand Meaulnes
57. **James J. Supple.** Racine: Bérénice
58. **Timothy Unwin.** Constant: Adolphe
59. **David Shaw.** Molière: Les Précieuses ridicules
60. **Roger Cardinal.** Breton: Nadja
61. **Geoffrey N. Bromiley.** Thomas's Tristan *and the* Folie Tristan d'Oxford
62. **R.J. Howells.** Rousseau: Julie ou La Nouvelle Héloïse
63. **George Evans.** Lesage: Crispin rival de son maître *and* Turcaret